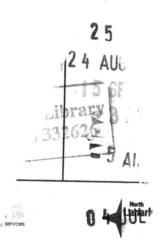

NOWHERE TO HIDE

JOHN McSHANE

NOWHERE TO HIDE

THE MOST EVIL CRIMINALS IN
BRITAIN ARE BROUGHT TO JUSTICE
BY AMAZING DNA TECHNOLOGY

JOHN BLAKE

Published by John Blake Publishing Ltd,
3 Bramber Court, 2 Bramber Road,
London W14 9PB, England

www.blake.co.uk

First published in hardback in 2008

ISBN: 978 1 84454 490 5

British Library Cataloguing-in-Publication Data:

A catalogue record for this book is available from the British Library.

Design by www.envydesign.co.uk

Printed in Great Britain by
William Clowes Ltd., Beccles, Suffolk

1 3 5 7 9 10 8 6 4 2

Papers used by John Blake Publishing are natural, recyclable products
made from wood grown in sustainable forests. The manufacturing
processes conform to the environmental regulations of the country
of origin.

Every attempt has been made to contact the relevant copyright-holders,
but some were unobtainable. We would be grateful if the appropriate
people could contact us.

CONTENTS

1

IN THE BEGINNING

The 140,000 motorists who race along the M1 in Leicestershire every day probably don't pay too much attention to the anonymous scenery that passes by in a blur. Perhaps if they pull off the motorway for a break they might peer out of the windows of Leicester Forest East service station towards the sleepy villages-cum-suburbs nearby as they sip their cappuccinos and plan the rest of their journey. Then, cups drained, they pass on their way.

Unknown to the vast majority of them, this unexciting hinterland was the setting for two murders so brutal they shocked the nation and brought fear to everyone who walked the nearby streets for years. The deaths started a groundbreaking manhunt, the like of which no country had ever seen. The crimes were eventually solved in a sensational manner that was to change forever the means by which a population can identify the perverts and criminals in its midst.

In the aftermath of those barbaric slayings a debate began which continues to this day on how a society can both protect itself from those who wish to damage it while retaining the right of an individual not to be placed on the ultimate Big Brother database run by the state.

All that lay years in the future when on the chilly, moonlit night of Monday, 21 November 1983, 15-year-old Lynda Mann got ready to visit her best friend Karen Blackwell. The frost was already beginning to appear on the ground as, at about 7pm, she headed for the door of her semi-detached council-house home in the village of Narborough. 'Don't worry,' she said to her mother, 'I'll be home by ten.'

Lynda arrived at her friend's soon afterwards, gave Karen's mother £1.50 towards a catalogue club the young girl was in, and then said she was off to another pal's home to collect a record. A little while later, having completed her circuit, she set off to take a dimly-lit footpath known as the Black Pad, near the cemetery behind the local church. The path ran alongside Carlton Hayes Hospital (formerly called by its almost-Dickensian name of the Leicestershire and Rutland Lunatic Asylum) but was separated from the hospital grounds by black iron railings. Young Lynda was never to be seen alive again – except by the man who killed her.

That night her mother and stepfather, Kath and Eddie Eastwood, went to a pub and spent the night playing darts. When they got home they were greeted with the words no parents want to hear late at night: their other daughter Susan told them Lynda wasn't yet home.

Eddie Eastwood immediately began to drive around the streets looking for her, but without success. He even looked down the Black Pad. By 1.30am, frantic with worry, the parents contacted the police. It was not unusual for a teenage girl to be out late at night, but the Eastwoods knew there was something seriously wrong.

Lynda Mann, just 5ft 2in tall and weighing a mere eight stone, was found early the next morning by a hospital porter on his way to work. She was in the hospital grounds on the other side of the fence from the path. The porter ran for assistance and returned quickly with an ambulance driver from the hospital, who immediately realised the girl was dead.

By mid-morning Eddie Eastwood was back at Black Pad for the heartbreaking task of identifying the young girl's body and that afternoon a post-mortem was carried out at Leicester Royal Infirmary. It found that she died from asphyxiation; she had been strangled to death. Crucially there were tiny traces of semen that could be taken for analysis and these were to play a key part in the events that would unfold.

The proximity of the hospital, with its numerous psychiatric patients, meant many leapt to the conclusion that it must be linked with the teenager's death. So much so that the hospital had to say 'Although this tragedy is right on our doorstep, there is no reason to suspect there is any connection with the hospital.'

The police headquarters were set up at the hospital, in an

unused Edwardian brick building originally designated for doctors to live in. House-to-house teams and a 'hospital squad' – who would focus on patients at the hospital – were immediately set up, making their base in the nearby pavilion adjoining the hospital cricket pitch.

They targeted the villages of Narborough and adjoining Enderby and Littlethorpe, filling out documents on every man aged between 13 and 34. These age ranges were chosen because the traces on young Lynda's body showed a high sperm count, which was indicative of a young man being the attacker. The hospital squad quickly realised that with out-patients and the day-care centre in operation, there would be literally thousands of men to look at.

By the middle of December, a month after the slaying, there had still been no breakthrough, although it was announced that £5,500 was to be spent on street lighting for the Black Pad. It was no wonder. The entire area was gripped with fear. The nurses at the hospital were scared to walk to work, and all women and girls nearby feared that as the killer was still at large, they could be his next victim.

By the fourth week of December the Eastwoods faced the awful prospect of a Christmas without their daughter, taken from them in terrible circumstances. Eddie Eastwood said: 'We live each day hour by hour, minute by minute. I just hope the man who killed our Lynda is suffering as much as we are. I just hope he's thinking about the damage he has done to our family while he celebrates his Christmas.'

Kath Eastwood said: 'This man has got to be punished and I hope anyone who knows him will think twice about harbouring him. We just do not have an existence any more and he is to blame.'

As the old year gave way to the new, there were still nearly 100 officers trying to find Lynda's killer. More than 3,000 statements had been taken and 150 blood tests from 'suspects' were analysed by the time she was buried on 2 February at All Saints Church, near the spot where her body had been found. But as the year wore on the number of officers involved was gradually reduced, and by August 1984 the official inquiry had come to a halt. It seemed the killer had escaped justice. The odds were that he would never be caught – unless he struck again.

If the murder of Lynda Mann was an example of the darkest, lowest side of the human character, an example of the higher achievements of mankind could be found only a few miles away from where she had met her death. Unknown to anyone at the time, it was to change the world in which we live.

The University of Leicester had been founded in 1921 and gained full degree-awarding powers in 1957 when it was granted its Royal Charter. Famous names associated with the university include actor Lord Richard Attenborough and his brother, the television naturalist Sir David Attenborough, the poet Philip Larkin, the authors C.P. Snow and Malcolm Bradbury, and the astronomer Patrick Moore. But 34-year-old Oxford graduate Alec Jeffreys, an expert in the comparatively new study of deoxyribonucleic acid (DNA), was to have an impact on society probably far greater than any of them.

Scientists James D Watson and Francis Crick, together with

Maurice Wilkins, had already received the Nobel Prize in 1962 for their work on DNA, the chemical inside the nucleus of a cell that carries the genetic instructions for making living organisms. Unlike Jeffreys, the pair were known in the mainstream world for their work and the knowledge it had given mankind. Before their discovery, scientists had only a vague notion about how human bodies store the information that dictates height, eye and hair colour, intelligence and most other attributes. Thanks to their understanding of DNA and, crucially, its double helix shape – like two spirals attached by an infinite number of 'rungs' – some scientists were able to perfect tests that could pinpoint hereditary flaws in the unborn, while others had genetically engineered bacteria to manufacture valuable drugs.

Nobel Prizes must have seemed a distant dream for genetics lecturer Jeffreys, a polo-neck sweater man with a liking for cigarettes rolled from Golden Virginia tobacco, and his team in autumn 1984, some ten months after Lynda's murder – a crime carried out just a 15-minute drive from the University's campus.

In later years Jeffreys, by then Sir Alec, was to recall the events of 9pm on Monday, 15 September, when he removed some X-ray film from the developing tank and experienced a rare moment in science. 'My first reaction was that the results were really yucky-looking and complicated. It took about 30 seconds for the penny to drop. I came rushing out of the darkroom. The first person I saw was Vicky Wilson, my technician. "Hey, we're on to something exciting here!" I told her. We started coming on to all sorts of crazy ideas. I was

6

running round the lab with a needle, pricking myself and spotting blood drops around, because at that point we didn't even know if DNA would survive in a forensic-type specimen. It was a 100 per cent accident. Science tends to be a slow, plodding discipline: two steps forward, one step back. To get a eureka moment like that, when suddenly an entire new field opens up, is really rare. Most scientists will go their whole lives never experiencing it.

'I thought, "My God, what have we got here?" but it was so blindingly obvious. We'd been looking for good genetic markers for basic genetic analysis and had stumbled on a way of establishing a human's genetic identification.'

He also recalled: 'We went in to read the X-ray from different blood specimens: there was a family group, some unrelated people, and some non-human animals – a chimpanzee, a lemur and I think a seal. It was totally staggering: I stood transfixed for five minutes. These wonderfully complex patterns were individual-specific. They could sort out family relationships, and applied across the species: human, seal, monkey. It was the key to unlock the door. Suppose we could test a million people every second. How long would it take to find one exactly the same? The answer is, the universe itself would die before we found one the same. It is simply an incomprehensible number. By the afternoon we'd named our discovery "DNA fingerprinting"'.

To understand how Sir Alec and his colleagues came up with DNA fingerprinting and subsequent enhancements of the technology, it's necessary to go back to the late 1970s, when they began a search for regions in human DNA that varied between different people. They hoped their work would enable them to map genes and develop diagnoses for inherited diseases. At that time, he was searching for variable bits of DNA in regions where the DNA code is repeated, or 'stuttered'. Each human chromosome is one long DNA molecule with four different chemical letters written down its length, tens of millions of times. If that almost endless string of DNA was examined, the letters would look random, but at certain points you'd hit segments where the sequence was repeated. If an ordinary segment of DNA read 'Humpty Dumpty sat on a wall' one of the stuttered segments would read 'Humpty Dumpty sat on aaaaaaaaa wall'.

'People had already stumbled over several of these stuttered regions of DNA purely by accident,' says the geneticist. 'We wanted to find a way to get to them any time we wanted.'

While continuing his work on stuttering DNA, he became involved in a side project looking at the evolution of genes. 'One of the genes we were interested in was myoglobin, a gene which produces the red pigment found in muscle. It's a relative of the gene which codes for haemoglobin, the oxygen-carrying pigment in blood. We knew that myoglobin had split from haemoglobin about half a billion years ago, so we thought it would take us back to some ancient events in gene evolution.'

When Sir Alec isolated the myoglobin gene, he found it contained 'stuttered' bits of DNA, plus a strong clue that these stutters occurred at particular chemical motifs within the DNA. There was also a suggestion that if these stuttered bits of DNA varied from one person to another, and if we developed a chemical probe which could latch on to this chemical motif that was shared between different stuttered regions in a person's DNA called mini-satellites, we could isolate a lot of stuttered DNA regions at once and thereby develop good markers for genetic analysis.'

Complicated stuff, perhaps, but the eureka moment was about to happen for the Jeffreys' team. When, on that early-autumn Monday morning, Jeffreys stood in his darkroom with some freshly developed X-ray film, he noticed not only had the experiment worked, in that he could see lots of the mini-satellites, but the pattern they made varied quite extraordinarily from one person to another.

Excitement mounting, Jeffreys and his team spent the rest of that morning discussing the practical implications of their discovery. 'In theory, we knew it could be used for forensic identification and for paternity testing. It could also be used to establish whether twins were identical and important information in transplantation operations.

'It could be applied to bone-marrow grafts to see if they'd taken or not. We could also see the technique working on animals and birds. We could figure out how creatures were related to one another – if you want to understand the natural history of a species, this is basic information. We could also see it being applied to conservation biology. The list of applications seemed endless and that's how it's turned out.'

By the afternoon all the team were pricking their fingers and smearing blood on tissues and bits of glass to see if they could produce DNA fingerprints from this evidence. They found they could.

'It was a classic case of basic science coming up with a technology which could be applied to a problem in an unanticipated way,' Sir Alec says.

The DNA fingerprint subsequently appeared as a pattern of bands or stripes on X-ray film, similar to the bands on a supermarket item's barcode. The technology's applications for forensic science were far-reaching: it could determine whether two separate biological samples came from the same person.

It could also be used to establish family relationships, because the banded patterns the technology produces are inherited. 'Half the bands from a child's DNA fingerprint come from its mother and half from its father. In paternity testing, you take the child's banding pattern and that of the mother and the alleged father. The bands on the child's DNA fingerprint that are not from the mother must be inherited from the true father. And no two people have the same DNA fingerprint, other than identical twins.'

This amazing discovery was soon put to practical use the following year, when it enabled a Ghanaian boy, 15-year-old Andrew Sarbah, to prove he was the genuine son of a couple in an immigration dispute.

The technology's limitations for forensic analysis soon became apparent, however. To begin with, a lot of good-quality DNA was required to obtain a good fingerprint and old DNA could degrade, which could cause problems at any subsequent criminal trial.

Another problem occurred if there was a long interval between the collection of a DNA sample from a crime scene and the taking of a sample from a suspect. 'The nature of the test means that the pattern, while completely reproducible in a single experiment, can subtly shift from one experiment to another,' Jeffreys points out. 'These patterns are not black and white like a barcode. They're grey codes with light and dark patterns. If you do a second test some time after the first, some of the faint bands might disappear or get darker.

'There's also the problem of aligning the two patterns for comparison. It can be done by eye, but that's not acceptable evidence in court.'

In 1985, the Leicester University team developed a method that overcame these limitations: DNA profiling. This enabled the isolation of individual mini-satellites and the production of a pattern on X-ray film with just two bands per individual – one from the person's mother and one from the father. As well as requiring a smaller DNA sample, it also meant the information obtained could be stored on a computer base.

If the world of academia in Leicester was beginning to absorb the praise and acclaim from the scientific world that the genetics team had brought it, in the outside world a fresh horror was about to unfold.

Dawn Ashworth was just 15 in the summer of 1986. The girl worked part-time during the school holidays at a newsagent near her home in Enderby to earn some extra money. But on the afternoon of 31 July she was free and decided to visit two friends in nearby Narborough, the scene of the murder of Lynda Mann (like Dawn, a pupil at Lutterworth Grammar School). Neither of Dawn's friends were in, so she headed back home, using a route near the motorway not too far from Carlton Hayes Hospital, known as Ten Pound Lane.

It had been almost three year since Lynda's death, but all the girls in the area were still aware of it and were advised to take care as they travelled around. But it was mid-afternoon on a summer's day so a walk down the tiny lane with its undergrowth nearby wouldn't have been too worrying for Dawn in her white skirt and white pumps.

When she had not returned home by 7pm, her parents, Robin and Barbara, began to worry. They contacted the parents of Dawn's friends and were told she had not been seen for some hours. They both looked around the area without success and wanted to call the police. Dawn had said in the past she would not stay out after 9.30pm and once that time had passed they promptly telephoned the police.

The next day the hunt began. Local police with tracker dogs scoured the area without success. Newspapers that Saturday carried a brief story saying: 'The parents of a Leicestershire schoolgirl who disappeared close to the spot where another teenager was murdered three years ago said yesterday that they feared she had been abducted. Dawn Ashworth, aged 15, was last seen leaving the home of her best friend, Sharon Clarke, in the village of Enderby, on Thursday afternoon. Her one-and-a-half mile walk home could have taken her along the edge of an area known as the "Black Pad" where Lynda Mann, also aged 15, was sexually assaulted and strangled. Her murderer was never caught. Both girls were pupils of Lutterworth Grammar School.

'Dawn's father, Mr Robin Ashworth, who was routinely questioned by police during their investigation into Lynda's murder, said: "We constantly warned her to be careful because there was a killer on the loose."

'Mr Ashworth, a scientific officer with British Gas, comforted his wife Barbara, who said: "Dawn will be absolutely panic-stricken by now if she is being held against her will. There is no way she would have gone away from home by herself."'

Dawn's body, semi-clothed, was found the next morning, a Saturday. It had been partially buried under a mound of foliage with leaves heaped on it in a field alongside Ten Pound Lane. She had been sexually assaulted and the indication was that she had been manually strangled to death – less than a mile from where Lynda had been found. The monster had struck again.

The officers who had worked without success on the first murder had feared that the man they were after would repeat the horror of that first attack, and now it had happened.

But if the hunt for Lynda's killer had been long and drawn-out without any breakthroughs, this time events moved at a much faster pace. There had been sightings of a young man with a red motor-cycle helmet in the area on the afternoon when Dawn disappeared, and a motor-bike was seen parked under the motorway bridge nearby. A youth, presumably the same one, was seen on the Friday, hanging around the area where her body was to be discovered the next day. Crucially the man, who turned out to work as kitchen porter at Carlton Hayes Hospital, was said to have mentioned to a colleague that Dawn's body had been found in a hedge near a gate by the M1 – hours before her body was actually found.

Six days after Dawn's body had been discovered, and with a local businessman offering a £15,000 reward for information leading to the capture of the killer, the police raided the Narborough home where the 17-year-old kitchen porter lived with his mother and taxi-driver father.

Under questioning the teenager gave a series of rambling, often incoherent and contradictory answers, but then said he was the man who attacked Dawn. It looked as though the police had got their man. He also mentioned sexual incidents with other young girls that the police checked out and verified, so on 11 August he appeared at Leicester Magistrates Court charged with Dawn's murder. But what about Lynda Mann? Surely the same pervert must have claimed the lives of both girls?

The youth vehemently denied killing Lynda, in spite of the many similar circumstances surrounding the girls' deaths, yet it seemed almost inconceivable that another monster was on the loose in such a small geographical area.

So it was that police decided to analyse again the semen sample from Lynda Mann and the blood sample from the kitchen porter. Surely there would be a match. And where better to go than the city's own university where the new genetic fingerprinting might solve a three-year-old riddle?

Like everyone in Leicester, Alec Jeffreys had read the details of the two murders. In September 1986 he analysed the somewhat degraded sample of semen from the Mann case and compared it with the blood of the kitchen porter. The results were sensational.

'I went through the analysis and proved that the semen samples obtained from both victims were from the same man,' Jeffreys would say. 'And the second point was that the samples certainly did not come from the man who was charged... If we hadn't developed the technology, I'm confident he would have been jailed for life.'

So the man under arrest was not the double killer. Not only that, he hadn't killed the teenager whose slaying he had confessed to! It meant that the police were back to square one. Well, not quite.

They now knew for sure that the same man had killed both girls and, more important, for the first time in the blood-soaked history of murder, they had a genetic fingerprint of their man. The problem they now faced was how to match this fingerprint with the killer, wherever and whoever he was.

First, the charge against the kitchen porter was dropped at Leicester Crown Court on 21 November and he left the building a free man. That afternoon Assistant Chief Constable Brian Pollard, flanked by Detective Chief Superintendent David Baker and Det Supt Tony Painter, called a press conference to explain how and why the young man had come to be released.

'Those tests did not implicate him in the murder of Lynda Mann. Further tests were asked for by the investigating officers on the murder of Dawn Ashworth. The tests were carried out and results were checked by scientists at the forensics science laboratory in Aldermaston, who confirmed the findings. The result of the test indicates that a person as yet unknown was responsible in the deaths of both girls. The Crown Prosecution Service have been kept informed and have decided that proceedings should be discontinued.'

No doubt many of the police who had hunted the killer were disappointed that the man they thought was the murderer was now free, cleared by the very procedure they had hoped would prove his guilt. Some probably still harboured the gut feeling that he was their man, no matter what the boffins might say.

But now senior police officers decided to embark on the revolutionary step that was to place the two girls' murders in the history books: they decided to use the very evidence that had proved one man innocent to prove the guilt of the killer they knew was still somewhere in their midst.

Christmas came and went and the New Year empty bottles were still lying around countless East Midlands homes when the sensational announcement was made. This is how *The Times* newspaper reported it the next day, 2 January 1987: 'About 2,000 men are to be asked to provide specimens of blood and saliva in an attempt to trace the murderer of two schoolgirls. The tests will be carried out in the Leicestershire villages where Lynda Mann and Dawn Ashworth, both aged 15, were killed a few hundred yards apart. Police have established a scientific test which provides a 'genetic fingerprint' of the man who killed the girls. The test has already proved that a man earlier charged with one of the killings was innocent. Both girls – who went to Lutterworth Grammar School – were sexually assaulted and strangled as they walked close to their homes.

'Dawn, who died in August, lived in the village of Enderby and Lynn, who was killed three years ago, in the neighbouring village of Narborough. Now males aged 16 to 34 in Enderby, Narborough and Littlethorpe, another village near by, are being asked to provide samples of testing. Police believe that one man murdered the two girls and they can corner the killer – or at least eliminate suspects – by the 'genetic fingerprinting' method developed at Leicester University.

'The 'genetic fingerprint' was developed by Dr Alex Jeffreys, of Leicester University, in association with the Home Office's central research establishment at Aldermaston. Known as DNA testing, it involves subjecting body samples to detailed microbiological analysis. The manner of identifying the person involved is as individual as a fingerprint taken from the hands. The method involves samples of blood, saliva or semen and was used by detectives in Leicestershire when they decided to take no further action against a hospital porter who had been charged with the murder of Dawn Ashworth. Samples of fluid taken demonstrated that he could not have been involved in the murders and he was released after three months in custody.

'Two local centres are being established for the tests to be carried out on the local male population.'

The flaw in this system was obvious: the tests were voluntary. If the killer was approached, the odds were that he would refuse to give a sample for fear of discovery.

Nevertheless the hope was that this mammoth task would in some way force the man out into the open, as all those who refused to participate would automatically set the alarm bells ringing among detectives.

The task ahead, however, was enormous. Although the blood test would automatically rule out some men, so that only a minority would proceed to the second stage of the DNA fingerprinting process, the administration involving the police, medical and forensic staff was immense. Soon a backlog began to build up.

The men who volunteered had to provide some form of identification – a passport was best, as these were the days before photographs appeared on driving licenses – and they then had to be taken to a doctor or medical staff who would take blood and saliva samples. These were then sent to a laboratory in Huntingdon for analysis and if that blood sample failed to rule out a man, it was passed on to the Government's Aldermaston laboratory for the genetic fingerprinting process to begin.

By the end of July no fewer than 4,195 men had given blood and, from the results received, 3,556 had been eliminated from the investigation. Det Supt Painter said of the one man who had not cooperated – but who turned out not to be the killer – 'We are still endeavouring to persuade him, but he is no more a suspect than anybody else. But without a blood sample, we have not eliminated him from our enquiries. A number of people refused to start with, but we saw them, explained the situation and they eventually agreed. It is a voluntary test'.

The fact that just one man out of more than 4,000 had not volunteered showed the tremendous depth of feeling in the area, where both police and public feared the killer might strike again at any moment. A further 400 men had still to be tested and police were trying to contact at least 20 who had left the area.

By this stage Leicestershire Police, who still had 24 officers on the case, had taken more than 7,300 statements since the investigation started in November 1983 and made nearly 25,000 entries on the computer being used. Three quotes made at the time summed up the mood of the police and the families of the victims:

Det Supt Painter said: 'Dawn was murdered on 31 July and we mean to use the anniversary to give the enquiry another boost. We know there's a risk that this evil man will strike again and we know that there's information in the community that could lead us to him.'

Lynda Mann's mother Kath Eastwood said: 'It's a process of elimination at the moment. I don't think they can do any more. I'll never give up hope and I'm sure they will find him in the end.'

And Det Chief Supt Baker summed it up: 'As a result of the scientific progress of the case, we can state quite categorically that the person involved in the death of Lynda Mann was also involved in the death of Dawn Ashworth.' But even he had to concede: 'We have not got that vital piece of information which would allow us to put the jigsaw together. Somewhere, someone may hold a piece of information, perhaps about somebody's movements, which would help us.'

Little did he know how near at hand that help was. It came in the shape of bakery manager Jackie Foggin who, at around the same time that the police were renewing their appeal, was having a lunchtime drink with colleagues at a Leicester city centre pub. As they were talking, one of the men in the group, Ian Kelly, let slip that he had taken 'that' test on behalf of one of the bakers, a young man called Colin Pitchfork. Another man in the group then remarked that Pitchfork had earlier asked him to take the test too, but he had refused.

Mrs Foggin, 26, couldn't forget what she had heard and it preyed on her mind. Some weeks later she eventually made contact with a policeman who was related to the manager of the pub and told him what she'd heard.

As soon as the officers involved in the double murder hunt heard the details from that pub conversation, they checked out 27-year-old Colin Pitchfork and discovered two signatures of his on documents they had in their possession. One was from the original Lynda Mann enquiry, when he had been routinely questioned as he lived in Narborough. He hadn't been living in the area at the time of that murder, and as he had only moved there after Lynda's death, no further action was taken against him. But he'd signed the form the police had presented to him during their brief questioning and they now compared it with the recent test he had supposedly given as part of the mass genetic-fingerprinting campaign. The two signatures were not the same. The reason was simple: Ian Kelly had taken the test instead of Pitchfork.

The story was reaching its dramatic conclusion. Kelly was seen first and confessed to what he'd done. Pitchfork had given him a passport altered so that Kelly's picture was in it. Kelly had learned to imitate – or so he thought – the baker's signature and he'd learned family details such as his date of birth and names of his family. Pitchfork – who'd realised the DNA would trap him – had told colleagues a variety of stories to get them to stand in for him. He'd said he was scared of the police. He'd once been arrested for 'flashing' (exposing himself) and feared police would frame him.

The police then went to Pitchfork's house in Littlethorpe and arrested him in front of his astonished wife, Carole, who knew nothing of his crimes. He knew the game was up and confessed straight away. By 30 September his DNA specimen had been analysed and it confirmed that there was no false confession this time.

On 22 January 1988, Colin Pitchfork made legal and criminal history. Although DNA evidence had already started to be used in courts – at Bristol a 32-year-old labourer had been jailed for eight months for raping a 43-year-old woman after the court heard his blood sample provided a match for samples left on the woman – there had never been a case like Pitchfork's. He was the first man in the world to be convicted of murder based on DNA evidence. The likelihood was that without it, he would never have been caught for Lynda and Dawn's murders. And who might his next victims have been? The fear that he would have struck again was reinforced by the brief evidence the court heard that day.

Pitchfork pleaded guilty to the rape and murder of Lynda Mann, and to the murder of Dawn Ashworth. He also admitted two charges of indecent assault and one of conspiracy to pervert the course of justice. The father of two sons, he had dropped off his wife at an evening class before attacking Lynda. Incredibly, his baby son was asleep in the back of his car nearby while he attacked and killed her. After the murder he coolly collected his wife, showing no signs of what he had done.

Mr Brian Escott-Cox QC, for the prosecution, described the events leading up to the court hearing, saying that in August 1986, after Dawn Ashworth's killing, a 17-year-old from Narborough, Richard Buckland, was seen lurking near where she died. He was arrested and police were convinced that the same local man had killed both girls. In October, samples of the killer's semen taken from the girls, and blood from Buckland, were sent for analysis. Mr Escott-Cox said: 'The answer which came back was not the one the police expected. Undoubtedly the same man raped both girls, but it was not Buckland'.

Proceedings were dropped, Mr Escott-Cox told the court, and the murder incident room was re-opened. All males aged between 13 and 30 from the adjoining villages of Enderby, Narborough and Littlethorpe were asked to provide blood samples for genetic fingerprinting. More than 5,000 males responded and only two refused. One had a genuine reason; the other was Pitchfork. Three times in January appointments were made for him to give blood sample and twice he did not turn up. The court was told he had started pestering workmates to take the test for him, offering one £50 and another £200. Finally, Ian Kelly had agreed. After Kelly had revealed what he had done to workmates and one of them told police, Pitchfork was then arrested, said the prosecutor.

Pitchfork, who also admitted indecently assaulting two other girls, was sentenced to two terms of life imprisonment for each murder and 10 years each, to run concurrently, for raping the girls. Kelly, who admitted conspiracy to pervert the course of justice, was jailed for 18 months, suspended for two years, after the court was told he did not know that he was shielding a killer.

Mr Justice Otton told Pitchfork he was a dangerous man and would not be released for many years. 'What is disturbing is that had it not been for scientific detection by DNA you might still be at large today and other women would be in danger. This not only identified the murderer but removed suspicion from an innocent man. It is to be hoped that if such techniques have to be employed in the future the public will cooperate in a similar manner and lead to the detection of criminals.'

The judge's remarks encapsulated the virtues of genetic fingerprinting. Not only had it caught a guilty man, it had enabled an innocent one to walk free – a man who might otherwise have spent years behind bars. The debate on DNA was only just beginning, but one thing was for sure – crime-fighting would never be the same again.

2

THE BODY IN THE SUITCASE

The silver-grey suitcase was first seen on 2 November 2001, lying in the undergrowth of a thorn hedgerow near the minor road linking the busy A64 to the village of Askham Richard, four miles from York. A barman at a nearby pub, The Buckles Inn, tried to move it but it was too heavy. It was rigid, smart, had an extending pull-out handle and wheels, and most importantly, it was large enough to hold a vast amount of luggage. The barman mentioned it to a friend, a policeman who lived some distance away, and the officer advised him to report it, but he didn't. So, for over two weeks motorists, cyclists and pedestrians who glimpsed the bag continued on their way, allowing the weeds and leaves to wrap their ever-growing camouflage around the case.

Eventually, on Saturday 17 November, an inquisitive local man, Paul Barlow, saw the case as he walked to catch a bus to York. He didn't touch it but the next day he returned on his bicycle to examine it – only to find it was so heavy he couldn't move it. He was alarmed that it weighed so much and, realising something was wrong, decided to call the police.

The officer who arrived that afternoon, PC Champion, noticed a smell of decay as he tried to move the case onto the roadside. The men managed to open it slightly and inside they saw a gruesome sight: what appeared to be an eye and some hair. Around the edges of the case they noticed blood and, as they tried to open it more, they could see human feet inside. Realising he mustn't disturb the evidence, the policeman snapped the case shut and a forensic team was immediately called in as darkness descended. The area was sealed off to traffic, with the police refusing at first to say why.

It was the beginning of a double-murder investigation that spanned the globe, uncovered callous theft and involved internet detection. It also had remarkable strokes of good fortune and was finally a memorable, painstaking example of police work that was to put an evil killer behind bars.

It wasn't until noon the next day that, in an attempt to preserve as much forensic evidence as possible, the suitcase was opened in the sterile environment of the mortuary at York District Hospital. The team carrying out this grim task were greeted with an appalling sight. Inside the case – measuring 29cm by 50cm by 72cm – was the body of a woman of Asian or Oriental origin. She had brown eyes, shoulder-length dark hair, wore plastic contact lenses and, although she had pierced ears, had no earrings, studs or jewellery on her. Nor were there any visible injuries to the slightly built young woman, just 4ft 11in tall. She had been bound and gagged before being put in the suitcase and her body was already beginning to decompose.

The post-mortem examination by Home Office pathologist Professor Chris Milroy failed to discover how the woman died and further forensic tests were ordered in an attempt to establish the cause of death, and whether she had been dead or alive when crammed into the case.

The woman had no distinguishing marks on her body and detectives had one massive hurdle to overcome as they started their hunt for her killer – who was she?

Detective Chief Inspector Alan Ankers, who was leading the inquiry, said North Yorkshire Police had asked every force in Britain to check their missing persons files to see if they contained a woman fitting the description. 'We have a female who has been, in effect, dumped on a country lane. She is bound and gagged and she is in a suitcase.' He added, in an unintentionally macabre understatement: 'Clearly, we are treating this as a serious incident.'

The police did not know how long the woman had been dead, but he said: 'It is quite possible that the suitcase and the body have been at the scene for some time and we are looking for the public, especially local people, to help us by coming forward with any information. We are particularly appealing to people who walk their dogs or ride horses in that area.'

Even as he was speaking, the minor road near where the

suitcase had been found was still cordoned off as officers carried out a fingertip search of the area. They also made house-to-house inquiries at the villages of Askham Richard – best known for its women's open prison, Askham Grange – and Bilbrough. Twenty-five officers were put on the case and an incident room was set up at York.

First enquiries by detectives suggested that the suitcase had originally come from South Korea. It contained a label with the word 'Genova' on it and the letters ABS as well as the number 493-4615 and a series of Oriental characters.

'This is a horrendous crime,' Mr Ankers said. 'Nobody deserves to end their life as an anonymous body stuffed in a suitcase and dumped in a hedgerow. We intend to find whoever was responsible. We are still anxious to establish how long the suitcase was lying in the bottom of the hedge and I am renewing my appeal to local people who used that lane at the end of October and the beginning of November this year to contact us.'

A few days later the first of many bizarre twists that lay in store emerged when it was revealed that the woman's body had been bounded and gagged using rare adhesive tape. Only 1,500 rolls of the exclusive £4.50 tape had been made and sold since December the previous year. The colourful tape, designed by fashionable London artists Gilbert and George, was about 50mm (2in) wide and bore a pattern of men's faces on a blue background. It was sold only at the Tate Gallery and the Tate Modern in London, and the Tate Galleries in St Ives, Cornwall, and Liverpool.

Another officer in the hunt, Detective Inspector Jon Reed,

said that because of the investigation the tape had now been withdrawn from Tate Gallery shops. 'One of those 1,500 rolls is critical to this investigation, and we would appeal to anyone who is or was in possession of a roll of this tape or who knows the whereabouts of any of this tape to contact us if only for elimination purposes,' he said.

Detective Chief Inspector Ankers admitted the identity of the woman still remained a mystery, although about 50 possible names had been suggested by other police forces or the public. A cause of death had still not been established and the results of forensic tests were not expected for several weeks, but the police had obtained details of the suitcase. 'The manufacturers have confirmed there is no regular outlet in the UK,' he said. 'The majority are for domestic sale in South Korea with a small percentage sold in Lebanon. We don't know if this increases the possibility that the victim is from South Korea and we may not know until we receive further reports from the pathologist.

'At the moment the earliest sighting of the suitcase in the bottom of the hedge comes from a local resident who puts it at the scene on or about the second of 2 November. We still want to hear from local people who have used that lane at the end of October or early November.'

Consultant forensic anthropologist Dr Sue Black of Glasgow University, who had given expert evidence to the international war crimes tribunal in The Hague, was called in to help. In December she revealed that the unidentified body was that of an Oriental woman, most likely from the East and South China Sea regions, and aged in her late twenties.

Detective Chief Inspector Ankers emphasised that the police's main priority was still to establish the identity of the victim. 'This report from Dr Black is a significant step forward, as we have now narrowed the search parameters both in terms of her ethnic origin and her age. As we narrow down the potential matches, it will enable us to concentrate on more dedicated lines of inquiry. We are still awaiting reports, evidence and opinion from other scientific specialists and I expect they will take us further forward in due course.'

By this time detectives now believed that as few as 850 rolls of tape had been sold, compared to 1,500 rolls as first thought. A disappointed Mr Ankers said: 'The tape is crucial to the inquiry, but the response from the public has been quite poor. We are still appealing to everyone who has bought this tape, or had it in their possession, to contact us at the incident room.'

As the hunt intensified, a motorist said he had seen a man near where the suitcase was discovered in the early hours of 2 November and detectives issued a description of a man they believed could help. He was white, in his late thirties or early forties, about six feet tall with a thin face, scruffy dark brown hair and he had heavy stubble. He wore a bulky ski-type waterproof jacket, dark jeans and black gloves and was driving a dark saloon.

But the big breakthrough the detectives had hoped for took place when the victim was identified. In France friends of a young Korean woman, Hyo Jung Jin , had voiced their concerns to the South Korean Embassy and to her family. Although signed up for two months of French lessons at the

Alliance Française in Lyon, she had failed to return from a visit to London around the time of the All Saints Day public holiday in early November. Her brother in South Korea was concerned enough to post her details on a website and, by a remarkable coincidence, a South Korean policeman, Byung-Ho Im, studying criminal justice at Leeds University, noticed the website page with her details on it.

Mr Im, a 38-year-old superintendent in the South Korean police force, first became interested in the case after seeing reports on TV news at the time of the body's discovery. During his search of websites used by Koreans living in Europe he saw the appeal from Hyo Jung Jin's family and immediately made the connection. Mr Im contacted the family in Seoul, who agreed to send him dental records, fingerprints and more pictures of the missing woman. With the help of the Korean Embassy, Mr Im obtained all the additional fingerprint information North Yorkshire Police needed. Her identity was confirmed because South Koreans who leave to study overseas must provide a set of fingerprints before departing. Detective Chief Inspector Ankers' team matched the fingerprints of the victim to Hyo Jung Jin's and a crucial part of the mystery was solved.

Miss Jin, the daughter of a retired policeman, was from a Catholic family who lived 25 miles southwest of Seoul in the Junju-Si province district. Heartbreakingly, all her father could say was: 'I cannot believe what happened to my daughter. All her friends who went abroad together for language study have come back already. But my daughter… I don't know what to say.'

Detective Chief Superintendent Ian Lynch said: 'We know the victim intended to travel to see the Korean community in London and officers are working closely with the Metropolitan Police. The priority is to establish her movements in the UK. Anyone who saw her in London or knows about her movements should contact us. We do not know her reason for wanting to visit London, whether it was to see friends or as a tourist. Above all, we need to know how her body came to be on the outskirts of York.'

The answer to that question came after the police in Yorkshire were contacted by Scotland Yard officers investigating the disappearance of another Korean woman studying in London, to see if there were any similarities.

A hotel management student at Guildhall University, In Hea Song, 22, had been reported missing by a friend on 18 December. Song had last been heard from 12 days earlier when she had gone on a short sightseeing trip and rung the friend on her mobile telephone, telling him she was near Tower Bridge. She was, naturally, of Oriental appearance, about 5ft 4in tall, of slender build with brown eyes and dark, shoulder-length hair. Importantly, she had been staying at an address in Augusta Street, Poplar, East London.

A Metropolitan Police spokesman said: 'Although there is no evidence to link the two incidents at this stage, we are keeping an open mind and will continue to work closely with officers from North Yorkshire Police.' That 'no evidence to link' phrase was very quickly replaced by a very strong link indeed, and one that was to solve a case that only a few weeks earlier had looked the toughest of nuts to crack.

North Yorkshire Police were now busy working with French detectives to investigate claims that large amounts of cash had been withdrawn from Hyo Jung Jin's bank account after she left Lyon on 21 or 22 October. Some 18,000 francs (about £1,800) was taken out in six instalments on one day in London. On 2 November, a further 5,000 francs (around £500) was withdrawn in four instalments in Paris.

North Yorkshire Police sent a team of 12 detectives to London to work with officers from Scotland Yard to establish whether the murder and the second student's disappearance were linked. Their inquiries centred on the living arrangements of the two women and the longer In Hea Song was missing, the greater the concern for her safety became.

Reports in Korean newspapers gave the first public indication that police might have a suspect, a Korean man named only as Kim, with whom, police thought, both women had lodged at one time.

Detective Chief Inspector Vic Rae said: 'We are really fearful for Miss Song's safety and we urgently need anyone who knows her whereabouts to contact police. She did not contact her family over Christmas or the New Year period, which is very unusual. She is from a very responsible family and her parents expected to hear from her. They are very worried. We are currently looking at a number of common denominators in the two investigations and the backgrounds of both women.'

Both women, who apparently did not know each other, had stayed at a flat used by Korean students in East London. Miss Jin stayed there for three days in October, while Miss

Song stayed for a week in November. Police said they were keen to interview the 31-year-old owner of the property, known as Kim, who went missing in mid-December. Ports and airports were alerted as the police hunted a man they now feared was a double killer.

Detective Superintendent Peter Ship of the Metropolitan Police's Serious Crime Squad, who was by now leading the investigation, said that CCTV footage showed Miss Song took a bus to York from London's Victoria station on 16 November arriving at 4.10am next day. She had returned to London after 12 hours, shortly before the body in the suitcase was found.

By now detectives had been told that Miss Jin had died from 'upper airway obstruction' – suffocation – and they had discovered that in her last email, sent at around 7pm on 26 October to South Korea, she said she had met a man who was 'kind' and had shown her the sights of London. She also said a lot of her money had gone, but she was planning to meet up again with her new friend in Paris to go to EuroDisney. The emails had then stopped, although she had previously been in touch almost daily, and that final message had been sent from a computer in the house where she was staying in London.

At last the full name of the man police wanted to question, Kyu Soo Kim, 31, was released. A Korean, he had rented rooms to the two women in a two-bedroom flat in Eagle Street and a maisonette in Augusta Street at different times during late October and November. Within days he was arrested. After being in Canada for a month, he was picked up in an internet café in London's exclusive Bond Street on 17 January. Three days later he was charged with murdering Miss Jin.

On 28 January he appeared at the Old Bailey charged with her murder and was remanded in custody until 25 March, but before that date was reached came another dramatic development.

While Kim was in custody, the hunt for Miss Song was continuing. Police soon released security-camera footage of her taken in central London moments before she had boarded a coach heading to York. They hoped these images might jog the memories of fellow travellers and wanted to hear from anyone who spoke to her on the journey or knew why she visited the city. Detectives had also been looking into Miss Song's financial records to see if her credit card has been used. The security-camera footage showed her withdrawing money from a cash machine moments before boarding the coach. She arrived in York at 4.10am the following day and stayed in the city for about ten hours before catching a coach back to Victoria.

Detective Chief Inspector Rae said: 'We are extremely anxious to trace anyone who may have spoken to Miss Song on the coach to York or when she returned to London Victoria. We would also like to hear from anyone who may know why she had visited the city and what she did while there. Mr and Mrs Song have had no contact with their daughter since 4 December last year and are now desperate for anyone who knows her whereabouts to come forward.'

In a statement, her father Gilyong and mother Nyoungouk

made an emotional appeal for information: 'We miss In Hea so much. Ever since her disappearance our friends and family have been waiting for news of her whereabouts and longing for her to return. It's hard to imagine what it's like to lose somebody you love and we desperately need help in tracing where she might be and if anyone knows anything about In Hea please let us know or contact the police.'

Concerns for her safety were growing daily and investigating officers must, in their hearts, have feared the worst. Even they, however, could not have anticipated the next gruesome discovery.

On 14 March a plumber was working on a house in Augusta Street. The home had just been bought by a young couple and plumber Paul Milne was busy fixing a sink in the bathroom when he saw bluebottles and other insects crawling in and out of a crack in the panelling at the side of the bath. He remembered reading reports of police searching the house, so he decided to call them.

On that occasion, 9 January, the police had found clothes but no trace of the missing young woman. When they arrived early on 15 March they now knew where to look. Removing the panel, they saw there was a hidden, sealed compartment below the bath. For hours they tried to open it and when they succeeded they at first found a pile of stinking clothes and two pairs of shoes. Then they also found the naked body of a young woman wrapped in a duvet. DNA tests on the corpse confirmed what everyone feared, that it was poor Miss Song. Like her compatriot she had been bound and gagged and had died from suffocation. Miss Song had stayed in the house in November, Miss Jin had been there the month before.

Kyu Soo Kim was soon charged with the second murder and in May he appeared at The Old Bailey where he denied both charges and was remanded in custody to await trial.

When the trial eventually began in early March 2003, the packed courtroom head how the two doomed women were 'murdered in the most chilling and distressing of circumstances'. Prosecutor Jonathan Laidlaw described the macabre method used to end their lives: 'When almost naked and in a state of undress the victim was bound with packing tape around the wrists and then packing tape was wrapped tightly round the lower part of the face, covering the mouth and nose and, unable to breathe, they suffocated to death. I am afraid each of these young women appears to have been alive when this took place. One hopes their suffering didn't last for too long.'

Mr Laidlaw said that Kim had killed both women and had drawn money out of their bank accounts using their cash cards after their deaths. 'This could only be achieved if the PIN numbers were known. This would indicate the killings were also deliberately extended so that information could be extracted from the victims before they eventually died.'

Although Kim had been described as 'seductive', Mr Laidlaw said that if there had been any sexual activity neither victim showed any signs of a sex assault and no semen was found. The motive could have been financial, he added, as the defendant was massively in debt and had borrowed money from one of the tenants of two properties he let to

Korean students visiting the country – one in Eagle Street, Holborn and the maisonette in Augusta Street, Poplar.

Mr Laidlaw also offered a more sickening possibility: 'It could be suggested that he achieved a sadistic form of pleasure from the form of killing, which was so slow and deliberate.' Any sexual or financial motives could have simply been incidental.

Miss Jin, he said, went on a sight-seeing trip to London from France and stayed at the defendant's address in Eagle Street and was last seen alive on 26 October. 'It seems likely,' said Mr Laidlaw, 'although it's impossible to be precise, that at some point during that evening when the defendant's girlfriend and others were away from the flat, she was murdered.' He said Jin's blood had been found on the carpet and walls of the bedroom where she slept, which suggested it was here that she was killed. Her body had been forced into a large suitcase and more blood had been found on a carpet in the bottom of a wardrobe in the bedroom where it appeared the suitcase had been stored.

On 30 October 2001 the killer hired a Peugeot car from a firm in Camden, North London, and headed north up the M1. When he returned the car it had done 655 miles which was sufficient to have made the 424-mile round trip to the country lane near Askham Richard where the suitcase was dumped. He said a forensic examination had revealed Jin's blood in the boot in the same sort of pattern as had been found in the wardrobe. 'There can be no dispute that the defendant used that car to take the suitcase with Jin's body in it up to North Yorkshire.'

Mr Kim gave the impression he was well-off but he was

deep in debt at the time of the murders, Mr Laidlaw added, saying the Korean owed thousands on defaulted bank accounts, credit cards and loans from friends. Kim fled to Canada, paying for the flight with his second victim's cash.

The evidence against the accused man was considerable, and soon he changed his plea to guilty to manslaughter in the case of Miss Song, but the prosecution refused to accept it and the charges of murdering both women remained against him.

As the trial continued, it emerged that at one stage the anxious mother of Miss Jin had spoken to the landlord, who had told her not to worry. Prosecutor Sallie Bennett-Jenkins read a police statement from Mrs Jin which recounted a telephone conversation with Kim, made a few days after Miss Jin went missing, when she became concerned over her daughter's whereabouts.

Mrs Jin said Kim had told her that her daughter had come back to the flat where he was sub-letting a room to her, accompanied by three Korean students, and had said they were going travelling, and that he had taken them to Victoria train station the next day. But Mrs Jin told Kim that he could not be telling the truth as a withdrawal was made from her family account from a London cash machine on 30 October – after the alleged journey to Victoria. 'Kim told me not to worry and even comforted me. He said she had probably decided not to go yet and that is why she had not been in touch.'

Soon there was more evidence for the jury to hear about two of the key elements of the case: the Gilbert and George tape and the large suitcase in which the first victim had been found.

Mariko Ishimura, the accused's girlfriend, said she had

asked Kim not to make general use of the Gilbert and George tape, which she had bought at the Tate Modern gallery in London and had hidden away. 'I treated the tape as special. He seemed to be using it as normal tape. I hid it, but it was not where I put it, so presumably he might have found it,' the 23-year-old Japanese hairdresser told the jury.

Then a friend of the accused, Hyung Gun Kim, told the Old Bailey he went to a department store with the defendant to buy luggage. Mr Kim, no relation of the defendant, said: 'He suggested that we go and have a look at some suitcases. I asked him why, and he said Mariko had a lot of belongings and he was going to get a suitcase for her.' He claimed Kim told him he needed a 'big suitcase' but, he said, they gave up because the baggage they looked at was too expensive.

A pathologist told the court that Miss Jin died a 'very unusual death' when she was suffocated in a mask of tape. Professor Christopher Milroy said that he had never personally come across the extremely rare way the 21-year-old had died, but had encountered it during a professional presentation in America. It was not unique, he told the jury, but 'very, very unusual'.

More details of how money was taken from Miss Jin's accounts were revealed by prosecutor Sallie Bennett-Jenkins. On 30 October, she said, at just after 2pm, £1,990 was withdrawn from her bank account in the space of just over 30 minutes.

The seven transactions using her cash-point card occurred at an ATM machine near a McDonalds restaurant in Oxford Street. There were two attempts at further withdrawals.

They were rejected because of insufficient funds on the account. Bank records also show the same card was used in the same ATM machine on 27 October at 3.45am in the morning when an attempt to withdraw £250 was unsuccessful due to the incorrect PIN number being used.'

On 1 November, Miss Jin's Credit Lyonnais card was used in Paris to withdraw a total of 5,300 francs – approximately £530 – in four transactions. 'That represents the maximum that can be withdrawn in one day,' she added. Kim had paid a female friend to travel abroad to use the card to withdraw cash for him. The court also heard that on 31 October Kim paid £522, including a £300 deposit, in cash, to hire a Peugeot 405 until 6 November and that he subsequently returned it a day early and was refunded his deposit.

Kim had used the journey to dispose of the suitcase with Jin's body in it, and the court was to hear that even while police in Yorkshire were trying to identify her, the landlord was desperately trying to prevent the discovery of his second victim's corpse.

A fellow tenant at Augusta Street, student Eun Gyo Moon, told the jury she was seconds from discovering the body of her murdered flatmate when Kim rushed to stop her. She was tidying her apartment when she tried to force open a cupboard only for Kim to pounce on her, telling her it could not be opened. Miss Moon said she had arranged to take over the rental of the property in November 2001, only days before Kim killed Miss Song.

Miss Moon said: 'I had to go back to Korea and I came back to London on 9 December. I had left my belongings with Kyu Soo (Kim) and he had agreed to look after them for me at the flat. I gave him £900 or £1,000. I spoke to In Hea on the phone while I was in Korea. She seemed to be in a very good mood. When I got back to Augusta Street, Kyu Soo answered the door, but In Hea wasn't there. He said he hadn't seen her for about a week. She said she wanted to put shoes in a cupboard, but her landlord stopped her, saying the door was jammed.'

Miss Moon also said that several days later Kim had become angry after being phoned by relatives trying to trace the other missing student, Miss Jin.

In his defence of the accused man, William Clegg QC told the jury the prosecution's case against Kyu Soo Kim was fatally flawed. 'I venture that not one of you can say to yourselves, "I know what happened". If you cannot answer that question now, at the end of the evidence, then the prosecution has not begun to prove how either girl met her death. We all know from the pathologists that each girl died as a result of her airway being obstructed by the application of tape to her face. But does any one of you know how that tape came to be applied to either of those unfortunate girls? What you know is that anyone who has their airway obstructed is going to fight literally like a drowning man in order to let the air get into the lungs. Yet in each case, the victims did not have one bruise between them. Do not shy away from the blunt truth of the case. Here we are at the close of the evidence and not one of you knows how the girls were incapacitated without causing any injury.'

Mr Clegg then said the Old Bailey jury should ask who was

present when they died. The prosecution suggested Kim was there alone. 'The central question is how could he alone have done it. Have the prosecution proved there was one person present at each death?' Unless jurors could answer that question, they could not 'begin to arrive at an adverse verdict against the defendant', he said.

Prosecutor Jonathan Laidlaw said Miss Jin could have consented to being tied up – but no one would ever know because Kim elected not to give evidence at his own trial. 'We don't have a clue what the defendant's case is,' Mr Laidlaw told jurors. 'What does he say happened to Miss Jin? Does he accept that he killed her and what is his defence to murder? There may have been consensual sex between he and Miss Jin – an element of bondage that went too far. Is he saying this is a terrible accident?'

Mr Laidlaw also said the reason Miss Jin's corpse was not physically marked may have been because she allowed herself to be tied up. 'She was last seen alive with this defendant in October 2001. Four-and-a-half hours later she was dead and in a suitcase. There was nobody else at the flat. Nobody broke into the flat. He killed Miss Jin.'

Forensic evidence – the DNA element of the case – linked her to the defendant's bedroom, not a room Miss Jin would have been expected to be in, he said.

'Then there is the nature of the tape used to bind Miss Jin. Only 850 rolls were produced for sale nationally and a roll of it was recovered from the defendant's girlfriend's flat. Can there be any doubt that the bindings came from this roll?'

Mr Laidlaw also reminded the jury Kim had bought a

replacement suitcase after disposing of Miss Jin's body and he then used her credit cards and lied to several people about her whereabouts.

Kim didn't enter the witness box during the trial, nor did he show any emotion when he was found guilty of both crimes. Judge Jeremy Roberts, who called it 'a Rolls Royce' investigation by police, told him: 'These were exceptionally wicked offences. You have snuffed out the lives of two young girls who trusted you and believed you to be their friend'.

In a joint statement by Detective Chief Inspector Alan Ankers, of North Yorkshire Police, and Detective Chief Inspector Vic Rae, of the Metropolitan Police, the officers said: 'We're extremely pleased with today's verdict. We wish to pay tribute to the entire team of officers whose determination and professionalism helped to secure this outcome today. We hope this result brings comfort to the family and friends of Miss Song and Miss Jin.'

But perhaps it is fitting that the final, more ominous, words should be from Detective Superintendent Peter Ship, the officer in charge of both murder inquiries. He said that while Kim – who was to serve at least 25 years behind bars – rented rooms to students in central London, he also travelled extensively in other parts of Europe, Southeast Asia and Canada. 'He committed two very similar killings here in a very short period of his life,' said Mr Ship. 'I cannot rule out that he has committed other offences in other countries.'

3

THE SATURDAY NIGHT STRANGLER

The remorseless certainty that DNA genetic finger-printing brings to solving crimes knows no boundaries – not even death. Many evil men who thought they had escaped retribution have been proved wrong as forensic scientists reach back into history and prove conclusively who has – or has not – carried out crimes.

Nightclub bouncer Joe Kappen was one such man. The father of three was eventually named and truly shamed almost three decades after he'd carried out a series of horrific murders of teenage girls which he felt confident he had got away with. Even more amazing was the fact that Kappen had been in his grave for 12 years before police were finally able to say he was the monster known as The Saturday Night Strangler.

The murders that were eventually to bring infamy to

Kappen had brought terror to South Wales in the summer of 1973, when 16-year-old hitchhiker Sandra Newton was found dead, her raped body dumped close to a local disused colliery at Tonmawr in the heart of a once-proud Welsh mining community. The last sighting of doomed Sandra was when she was walking home from a nightclub in the neighbouring town of Briton Ferry after a Saturday night out. Her chiffon scarf had been used to strangle her to death. One of the few clues was that an Austin 1100, one of the most popular cars of the time, had been seen 'going like the clappers' in the area at the time of the murder.

Her married boyfriend said that they left the nightclub together and had a 'quickie' in the back of an abandoned van, after which he then left her at the roadside and walked home in the opposite direction. This crude admission gave police a problem, so in public this act of intimacy was glossed over. There was still, however, a suspicion that the killer might be the boyfriend, but the murder hunt was to take another twist just three months later.

That September, 16-year-olds Geraldine Hughes and her close friend Pauline Floyd decided to hitch home after a Saturday night at the Top Rank Suite in Swansea, the favourite nightspot in that part of South Wales for youngsters wanting a good, old-fashioned night out. The girls worked together in a sewing factory earning £16 a week apiece and lived near each other in the villages of Llandarcy and Skewen, about seven miles apart. At 1am the girls decided to head for home. At that time of night the buses had stopped running and taxis were too expensive for two young girls who had to count every penny. Like many others they decided to hitchhike to Pauline's house in Llandarcy, where they would spend the rest of the night. They were never to reach their destination.

That night it began to rain and the two girls tried to keep dry by sheltering at a bus stop a few hundred yards from the club as they tried to hitch a lift. Motorist Philip O'Connor was sitting at traffic lights, listening to the radio, when he saw a white car swerve to pick them up. As he sat waiting at the lights, the car drew alongside him and he could see that both girls were talking to the driver, but they were preventing him from getting a good look at the man behind the wheel. All he could see was that the driver had a moustache and bushy hair.

A few hours later, at 10am on Sunday, with thousands getting ready for church, an elderly person walking near Llandarcy came across Pauline's body lying face down in a copse, with her black platform boots beside her. A 5ft-long rope had been curled around her neck several times strangling her, her head was battered and her clothes were heavily bloodstained. Fifty yards away was Geraldine's body, close to the busy main Jersey Marine Road which led directly to the M4. Like her friend she had a head wound and had been strangled with a rope from behind. The girls, both virgins, were clothed but examination proved conclusively they had been raped. As if their deaths could be even more grotesque, their killer allowed them both to get dressed after the sex attack – a fact shown by the fact that their feet were dirty inside their tights, meaning they had put them on after sex – and then he had killed them both.

And so began the biggest murder enquiry in Welsh history, with more than 150 detectives on what was dubbed the hunt for the Saturday Night Strangler. The police, under Chief Superintendent Ray Allen, set up a murder room in Skewen police station, relying, in those pre-computer days, on a complex manual card index system and a 'graticule' – a wall-sized white board divided into tiny squares in which individual inquiries or actions are listed and then crossed off when completed.

Passing motorists had said that a white car, soon identified as an Austin 1100 but without any registration number to track it down, was parked near the copse between 1.45am and 2.15am on the Sunday that the girls met their deaths. This was the detectives' best lead but it was one of the most popular cars on the road in those days and it transpired that there were more than 11,000 in use. In the early 1970s, they were all registered at their local taxation offices, not centrally. Every owner would have to be visited and a statement taken from them, including verification of their alibi if need be.

The Skewen murder room soon contained 35,000 index cards listing names and different subject categories – 'queer person', 'rumours', 'psychopath', 'psychics', 'pregnant women' and 'suspicious acts'. There were 10,500 'suspects', 11,000 car questionnaires, 4,000 statements from Austin car owners and 10,000 miscellaneous statements. The statistics and amount of paper involved was overwhelming.

To make matters worse, the final stages of the M4 were being completed nearby and hundreds of construction workers from all over the country had to be questioned. Detectives also had to crisscross the land in search of fairground workers as the murders had coincided with the annual Neath Fair.

Police issued posters urging girls not to hitchhike, and terror was stalking the Valleys. At a press conference Chief Superintendent Allen urged anyone who knew the killer to contact the police, saying: 'We are pretty certain he is being shielded by someone; could be a woman, could be a relative or someone close to him. That Sunday morning his shoes must have been muddy, his clothing could have been bloodstained. This man is sick and needs medical attention. He could kill again unless we can get him to a doctor. Let the police know about him before he kills again. We will look after him.'

Despite the urgency of his appeal, there were no rewarding leads. The hunt continued but it was beginning to lose steam. Time passed, and with the murder enquiry being wound down, the girls' clothing and the boxes of statements were shipped to Sandfields police station in Port Talbot, where they were to remain for almost three decades. Some were damaged by damp and mould as the years passed, but the most important material, the girls' underwear, was retained in dry storerooms at the Home Office's forensic science labs in Chepstow.

Over the decades, the case was reviewed and the odd suspect questioned, but it was more a formality than a serious investigation, and Kappen, as he carried on with his life in South Wales, must have thought that he had escaped.

The introduction of DNA fingerprinting didn't provide the breakthrough that police and the still-grieving families had hoped for, as the stains on the clothing weren't of sufficient size or quality to track down the assailant. It was the advent in the late 1990s of Low Copy Number DNA – capable of correctly analysing the most minute of specimens – that proved the key to solving the murders that were now over a quarter of a century old.

The girls' clothes went to a specialist research lab in Birmingham for the long and slow process of testing. The DNA of the girls and the man who attacked them had become mixed, which meant that scientists could get only a partial profile of the killer's DNA from Geraldine. But Pauline's results were much clearer and a full genetic profile of the killer was established: his genetic fingerprint had been found. But that did not solve the mystery: who exactly was he?

The National DNA Database held over one and a half million criminal profiles at that time, but none of them matched the killer's. In that sense, the police had to start from scratch again. So, in January 2000, Operation Magnum was launched to find the killer. It was 27 years after the terrible crimes had been committed, and at the time it was to be the longest period that any British crime – and perhaps any in the world – was to be solved after the deed was committed.

The Llandarcy murder room was recreated in the village of Pontardawe's police station, not far from the scene of crimes, with Detective Chief Inspector Paul Bethell and two detectives nearing retirement, Phil Rees and Geraint Bale, the small team involved. Their first task was to swab the most likely suspects. Although there was a list of 35,000 'suspects' it had to be narrowed down to the most likely 500 – because that was the largest number of swabs that could be obtained from the budget they had!

As well as DNA, the modern detectives had another weapon their predecessors hadn't: psychological profiling. They recruited Rupert Heritage, former chief of the behavioural science unit of Surrey Police, to draw up a 14-point profile of the killer. It predicted – with uncanny accuracy – that the killer would be white, unskilled, aged in his late twenties to mid-thirties, have a history of minor property crime, have come to the attention of the police as a juvenile around the age of 12, and was likely to live in the Neath area. Other telltale signs might be a history of assaults and possibly animal cruelty. He might have an absent father and a troubled marriage, and hobbies might include weapons.

In the months leading up to the murders there had been rapes reported in the Neath area, committed by a man wearing a balaclava and in which ropes had been used, a method similar to the one used in the murders. The rapist had waited for his victims and after grabbing them from behind, threatened them saying: 'Don't scream or struggle, or I'll kill you'. He bound their hands and asked: 'Are you a virgin?' The moustachioed, anorak-wearing man who stank of tobacco then raped each woman. He said to one terrified victim: 'Don't open your eyes. I'm going to have a cigarette and think about whether I'm going to kill you or not.' There was obviously a strong link between the two crime profiles, but there was no DNA available from those rape attacks so many years ago.

Drawing on the psychological profile, the team began the unenviable task of reducing their 35,000 list to 500. Their first eight months were spent purely going through files, knowing that even the tiniest slip-up, the smallest thing overlooked, could mean the killer would remain free. Mr Rees was later to say: 'No one outside the team ever believed we would get a detection from this. It was like throwing a dice for two years.' The police used criminal and tax records, the passport office and the Driving Licence centre to track down men, some as far away as New Zealand.

Over an eight-month period 353 men gave swab samples. None refused – it would have started alarm bells ringing if they had – but a great many of them were unhappy about being approached so many years on from the initial inquiry. 'Selling double-glazing must be easier than selling a DNA test,' said Rees'. 'It usually took two hours. The easiest people to deal with were those with convictions. They just wanted it out the way. We ended up swabbing in barges, taxis and hotel rooms. The worst was always their sitting room in front of the wife.'

Suspect 200 was at least a lot nearer home than New Zealand. He was Joseph Kappen and he lived on the Sandfields estate in Port Talbot. In the summer of 2001, Mr Rees made the short journey to the steel town and knocked on his door. Although Kappen's ex-wife, Christine Powell, was still living there, the man he wanted to speak to wasn't.

He had a very good reason for not answering the door – he'd died 12 years earlier. Mr Rees couldn't just take her word for it – he had to check with death records. Once this was established as true, Kappen was consigned to the 'dead pool': men who had to be crosschecked with DNA from their family before they could be eliminated – another long task.

Then at last, in the autumn of 2001, came a breakthrough. DNA specialist Dr Jonathan Whitaker managed to extract a profile from swabs taken from Sandra Newton's body. There was a three-way mix of DNA belonging to Sandra, her boyfriend and the killer. Sandra's killer had dumped her body in a remote, practically unknown, water culvert close to the disused Garth colliery, so police felt they were definitely looking for a local man, as a stranger wouldn't have known of its existence. The odds were, then, that police had at some stage spoken to the man.

The time that had elapsed since the murders was one of the main problems facing detectives, but at last it came to their assistance. There was a chance that the killer might, by this time, have had children who had reached adulthood and therefore might be on the national database if they too had turned to crime.

Because DNA is inherited half from the father and half from the mother, the riddle was on the point of being solved. Dr Whitaker knew therefore he now had 50 per cent of the killer's children's DNA profile. Starting with all the profiles submitted to National DNA Database by the South Wales Police, Dr Whitaker started searching for a version of the killer's profile by going through a ten-stage process, eliminating masses of suspects. Soon he had just 100 names whose genetic profiles were closely related to that of the killer. One of those names was of car thief Paul Kappen, just seven at the time of the slayings, but Kappen Senior was one of the names on the main list and immediately became the prime suspect.

Rees and Bale returned to Sandfields and Christine and her daughter Deborah gave DNA samples. By subtracting his ex-wife's DNA from her son's and daughter's, the forensic scientists would be able to recreate most of Joseph Kappen's DNA.

Mr Bethell later said that two weeks later: 'I was sitting at my desk in the Pontardawe murder room when the call came through from the forensic scientist, Colin Dark. He was going on about a partial match and the DNA banding. I said, "What are you telling me?" He said, "I think you've got your man". It was a strange feeling, very emotional. I don't get excited or overwhelmed, not after all these years. But I really did get a lump in my throat.'

What the forensic scientists had obtained was a three-quarters profile of Kappen identical to that of the Llandarcy killer which proved, from a statistical point of view, that he was the murderer. It wasn't enough, though: the police – and the dead girls' families – had to know for sure. On Christmas Eve 2001, Mr Bethell applied to Home Secretary David Blunkett to exhume Kappen's body. He was about to become the first serial killer ever to be pulled from the grave to establish his guilt.

Joseph Kappen had been a Port Talbot man, born and

bred. Born in 1941, he was one of seven children and had been raised by his stepfather after his parents' marriage broke up. He had also, as the psychological profile predicted, first been in trouble with the police at the age of 12. The following years were spent in and out of prison for minor crimes such as robbing gas meters, car thefts, burglary and assault. Tall and powerfully built – he worked-out with weights years before it became commonplace – he worked driving buses or lorries as well as being a nightclub bouncer. He also smoked cannabis and 20 Old Holborn roll-ups a day, as well as chewing tobacco through his nicotine-stained teeth. Not surprisingly, he didn't have any close friends and developed a reputation as a loner.

Kappen met his wife-to-be, Christine, on the beachfront at Port Talbot when he was 20 and she was 17. The couple married in 1964 but divorced in 1980. Only days after their wedding – with Christine already pregnant – Kappen was jailed for three years for breaking into houses to rob gas meters. In August 1965, Kappen was released on day parole to attend his grandfather Joseph's funeral and at the wake, with a warder downstairs, he dragged Christine into an upstairs bedroom and they had sex, making her pregnant again. By the time he was released he had two children he had never met.

Throughout the marriage Kappen would hit his wife – she thought it 'normal' behaviour – and force her to have sex with him. But she never thought to press charges and in those days domestic violence was something that the authorities often turned a blind eye to. Kappen even once strangled the family pet greyhound on a beach as he had decided it was too old to keep. He used wire he had picked up and throttled the dog in front of his frightened son.

Kappen – who liked to consider himself a ladies' man – had been seen by the police on 13 October 1973, nearly a month after the murders. They had been given his name by a retired Port Talbot detective, Elwyn Wheadon, who knew him and was aware of his violent streak. But Kappen claimed to have returned from Neath Fair at around 9.30pm on the Saturday and spent the rest of the evening looking after his canaries and then going to bed with his wife, which is where he stayed until about 10.30 the next morning. His wife backed him up, but was later to say: 'I alibied him but I always did whenever the police came knocking. You learned to do it without thinking. "On such and such a night he was with me, officer." I couldn't see him doing that. I cannot imagine him doing that to a child. I never saw any signs of an unusual interest in young girls.'

After his marriage break-up Kappen had become involved in a relationship with a local barmaid on the Baglan Estate, but the heavy-smoking bully contracted lung cancer and spent his final days in a wheelchair, hardly ever leaving home. He was 49 when he died in 1990.

Kappen was buried in Goytre Cemetery on the hillside on the outskirts of his home town, sharing a family grave with his stepfather Clemente Proietti and grandfather Joseph Herbert. All three coffins would have to be dug up – Kappen's was in the middle – and it was to take five months for permission to come through.

So it was that in the middle of May 2002, a team of police, forensic scientists, dentists and archaeologists began the gruesome task of exhuming the bodies. Although the weather that day had been fine, the digging was to take place at night under floodlights as the law insists that exhumations must be carried out at midnight to cause as little distress to the public as possible.

As work began under a large blue-and-white rented canvas tent, the heavens opened, there was a crack of thunder and lightning flashed as if in a Hammer horror film inspired by Edgar Allan Poe. Heavy rain began to fall as the team of white-clad investigators – including council gravediggers and health and safety officers – started their task. Mr Bethell said later: 'The heavens opened and thunder and lightning started, the like of which I have never seen. It was literally at the moment we came across the coffin of Kappen. There was a tremendous sense of foreboding. Is this evil being uncovered? I remember saying to the team, "He doesn't want to come up".'

The first to be lifted from the ground was his stepfather, then Kappen, and finally his grandfather. The coffins, all intact, were taken to a local mortuary where they were opened and scientists removed teeth and a femur from the leg, the likeliest sites for DNA to survive. Once extracted, the material was sent for DNA analysis and Kappen and his relatives were quickly returned to the hillside and placed back in the earth.

The results came through in less than a month, confirming what everyone connected with the case had suspected for some time: that Kappen was indeed the Saturday Night Strangler. 'To be honest, I was disappointed,' says Rees. 'It was a let-down. You're not going to pull him in. It wasn't like arresting him and taking him to a court of law.'

Perhaps the final words should lie with those anguished parents who had waited for years to know the truth. Geraldine Hughes's mother Jean – who, in 1976, had led a protest march of 50 of her sewing-factory workmates to 10 Downing Street with a 9,000-signature petition and handmade banners urging the restoration of hanging – was now 69. 'You know there are evils out there,' she said, 'but you never believe it will touch on you and yours. When it does, it is a lifetime's sentence of hell, believe me. Now we hope we can close the book on the most horrific chapter of our lives. Geraldine was full of life and gave us so much pleasure. She was the light of our lives and we have suffered the anguish, as any parent would, of asking ourselves whether we should have allowed her out that night. The area has been tainted with these murders for years and hopefully the stigma hanging over it will be removed once and for all. We are a close-knit community and though people have stopped talking about what happened, we know it is still a cancer in their thoughts.'

Her husband, retired oil-refinery worker Denver Hughes, 72, said: 'We have relived what Geraldine must have gone through every night for nearly 30 years. When we heard about the police breakthrough we couldn't believe it at first. We were so shocked my wife and I broke down and cried all night. We took flowers to Geraldine's grave and had a few quiet words with her and we felt we had put her to rest properly.

'The news about the police breakthrough gave us an overwhelming sense of relief. Our tears were the pent-up outpouring of emotions after so long. We cannot thank the police enough because they have never given up the hunt for the killer. It really is wonderful that technology has moved on to give police these vital new tools of detection.'

4

SARAH PAYNE –
A NATION'S AGONY

Sarah Payne was a bright-eyed eight-year-old who was enjoying the early days of the school holidays. She had gone out to play with her brothers and sisters in a country cornfield, an image of summer so English it could have featured on a tourist board poster. Yet soon Sarah's name was to enter the history books as one of the most pitiful victims of an attack the country had ever known, a crime that was to have social and legal repercussions far beyond the vile savagery it encompassed. It was also to be a case where the importance of DNA in tracking a criminal and – just as importantly – providing enough evidence to gain a conviction, was to be highlighted to a degree seldom seen before.

At about 7.50pm on that Saturday evening of 1 July 2000, Sarah was making her way out of the field at

Kingston Gorse, West Sussex, after playing with her brothers Lee, 13, and Luke, 11, and her five-year-old sister, Charlotte. They had all been in a cornfield a few hundred yards from their grandparents' home and the adults had left the boys in charge.

During their game Sarah, wearing her favourite blue dress and little black shoes, had hurt herself and ran back towards her grandparents' home. Lee did not manage to catch her up and watched helplessly as she ran through a gap in the hedge. By the time he reached the lane she had vanished. That was when Roy Whiting had spotted her. He hadn't been stalking her, he didn't know her or her family, he had no connection with poor Sarah at all. They just both happened to be in the same place at the same time.

No doubt Whiting had children on his mind that day. He always had, even though he was, amazingly, not classified as a paedophile, despite a savage attack on a nine-year-old girl some five years earlier. As in Sarah's case it had been a sunny Saturday and the girl had been playing, this time in the street. Whiting snatched the child, dragged her into his car and took her on a terrifying drive to a secluded spot in West Sussex. He then told her he had a knife and a rope, and ordered her to strip naked. He assaulted her and tried to force her to commit indecent acts before, after an hour and a half of this brutality, he allowed her out of the car. Sarah was not to be so lucky, if 'lucky' is the right word.

So it was that as Sarah set off to rejoin her family, she encountered Whiting. The back of his white Fiat van was almost like a sealed mobile prison with all the essentials for abducting and assaulting a child: a rope, nylon-tie handcuffs and Johnson's baby oil. He had spent the day cruising three parks, a funfair and a boating lake. It was after that, completely by chance, that Sarah met Whiting – a human being who truly was an accident waiting to happen.

Whiting was born on 26 January 1959 in nearby Horsham, but after his parents moved he grew up in Crawley, not far from the expanding Gatwick Airport.

Although he lived in a modern suburb, his was not a fairytale childhood. He was abused as a child by a close relative and his father George, a sheet-metal worker, was cautioned after an indecent act with a girl at the local swimming baths. In 1976 his mother left home on her daughter's 11th birthday leaving the three children – Whiting had an elder brother and younger sister – with their father.

Whiting – who was slow at school and a solitary child who never showed much interest in lessons – had one passion in life: cars. At 16, with few other options, he got a job as a mechanic, although even in the company of the other lads in the garage he failed to fit in. In the evenings he would spend his time doing up old cars at home and listening to heavy metal records.

From the mid-1970s until 1991 Whiting was a casual worker at the Cherry Lane adventure park in Langley Green, Crawley, where he would turn up and help children to fix their bicycles. He was also a member of the Crawley Tigers cycle racing team, which competed at the children's play area. He didn't appear to have any friends and lived some of the time with his father in return for doing jobs around the house. One day, after father and son had had a row, Whiting moved out and set up a home in a rented workshop where he had a job repairing cars. In this seedy abode the only furniture was a camp-bed, a kettle, a microwave oven and a TV. The decorations consisted of posters of racing cars on the wall. Were anyone looking for a snapshot to sum up Whiting's miserable life, it could be found here, behind the doors of his grubby little den.

Whiting was in his mid-twenties by this time. He told friends he'd had his first sexual encounter at 16 and progressed into several long-term relationships, but the truth was he probably exaggerated his sexual experience to appear normal. His hair was dirty and lank and his fingernails were always black and he washed by visiting the swimming baths once a week. It wasn't really surprising then that women showed little interest in him.

Then, to everyone's surprise, he married Linda, a Crawley brunette he'd first met in a local filling station where she worked on the till. His chat-up lines were hardly the most sophisticated in the world: he tried to impress her by making out a scar near his kidneys was a wound from a knife-fight. Linda would tell later how they 'drifted together', marrying in the summer of 1986 after she'd proposed to him. They had a son in 1987 – according to Linda, her husband did not bother to visit her in the maternity hospital – but separated the following year. 'In the end he simply walked out,' she said later. 'I came home one afternoon and he was gone.' Whiting sent money for their child for a few months but it quickly dried up, which meant the boy's contact with his father – on the rare occasions when there was any – was mostly through birthday cards or Christmas visits, or not at all.

Whiting did at least turn up at the divorce court in 1990, wearing a suit, although he still had oil and grime underneath his fingernails. The only thing that did seem to interest him was motor racing and he would spend days preparing his old Jaguar for banger-racing at the racetrack near Crawley, where his nickname was The Flying Fish. He even had that written on the side of his car. No one could remember him ever winning a race. Off the track he would eat all the time at a nearby café where he always ate the same meal: a hamburger washed down with two mugs of tea.

After being jailed in the mid-1990s for the attack on the nine-year-old girl, he made a rare contact with his ex-wife, writing from prison: 'I don't know why I did it'. In jail he pretended that he was imprisoned for car theft so he would not face the anger of his fellow inmates towards child sex-abusers. He even sat in on their rough-and-ready judgements of such 'pervs'.

In 1997, when he'd finished his prison sentence at Cambridgeshire's Littlehey jail, he told the warder who held the door open for him: 'I won't be coming back'. He might have meant it as a pledge to go straight, but the odds are he was merely informing them of his determination never to be caught again.

The white Transit-style van that Whiting bought six days before Sarah's abduction had been previously owned by a removal man who had fitted out the back with a plywood lining and partition to protect furniture. Whiting deliberately left it there so that any forensic evidence from encounters with children in the back could be ditched with the wood when he removed it. That was exactly what he was to do within hours of killing Sarah, before hosing it clean. In spite of his attempts to rid the van of the proof of his crime, however, it was to be evidence gathered from it that was to mean the end of the trail for this walking incarnation of evil.

The disappearance of Sarah was to horrify the nation. The adults in the family group in Sussex were told she had vanished and at 9pm, after a frantic 45 minutes of searching the area themselves Sarah's mother, Sara, dialled 999. When the police arrived Lee told them he had seen a white van speeding away from the lane describing the driver as a scruffy man with 'piercing blue eyes' wearing a workman's shirt.

Inspector Jeff Lister, the Worthing sector commander, was the first senior officer on the scene. He knew instantly that the signs were bad and a makeshift incident room was set up in the grandparents' conservatory. He phoned Detective Superintendent Alan Ladley, the senior detective on call, at home and he reached the scene by midnight. His team knew that time was of the essence and as every minute ticked by the chances of finding Sarah alive were diminishing. It is estimated that in 75 per cent of child abduction cases the victim is dead within hours. A massive search began and over the next 16 days more than 1,300 police officers hunted for Sarah, supported by many members of the public.

On the day after Sarah's disappearance, Detective Inspector Paul Williams, whose duties included keeping tabs on local sex offenders, drew up a short-list of the five most likely candidates to have taken her. Whiting, now 41, was top of the list.

That evening PC Chris Saunders went to Whiting's flat on St Augustine Road, Littlehampton, only to find he was out. When Saunders returned at 9.30pm, a white Fiat Ducato van was parked outside but Whiting insisted he had been at a funfair in Hove at the time of Sarah's disappearance. The rest of the evening he'd spent at home, he said. PC Saunders left but was uneasy and watched the house. 'What struck me was his blank expression,' he said. 'He wasn't overly concerned. He didn't show any emotions.'

The police watched as Whiting twice went to his van and removed items. When he emerged a third time he got into the van and began to drive away. It was now that the officers had to make an instant decision: whether to follow him in the hope he led them to Sarah or whether to arrest him there and then in order to stop him destroying evidence. They took the latter course and in doing so probably stopped him destroying the vital evidence that was to play a key part in his conviction.

In the van was a receipt for diesel that Whiting had bought at 10pm the night before from a garage at the Buck Barn crossroads, 15 miles north of Littlehampton and nowhere near the funfair. It later turned out that Whiting had insisted on a receipt, even waiting for the till-roll to be changed, a mistake that was to play a key part in the subsequent prosecution case. Also in the van were a knife, ropes, masking tape, plastic ties and a bottle of baby oil, which obviously made the officers suspicious. Apart from agreeing the van was his, Whiting had little else to say. He refused to explain scratches on his body and arms but as there was no solid evidence against him, he was released on police bail.

Police looking into Whiting's background established that he had done building work near Sarah's grandparents' house and that he had also walked a dog in the area. Importantly, on the Sunday after Sarah disappeared he had altered his van, removing panelling and changing the back doors.

Although he was an obvious suspect, police had to proceed on the grounds that he was innocent, so they interviewed hundreds of sex offenders throughout the country. Detective Superintendent Ladley later said: 'Every decision had to be made with the possibility that Whiting could be innocent.'

Sara Payne, 31, was soon to make an appeal that touched the nation's heart. It was on the Monday, barely two days after her daughter had vanished and as helicopters, a bloodhound, thermal imaging cameras, soldiers from the Royal Military Police barracks in Chichester and hundreds of volunteers joined the search, that she spoke out: 'You can't imagine what Sarah means to us. We're a strong family and we don't survive well apart. We need her home now, today, as quickly as we possibly can. Her brothers and her sister are really not coping very well without her. She's our life. Our family name for Sarah is our "little princess," and that's just what she is. She's just a soft, gentle little girl. She hasn't got a horrible bone in her body. Somebody out there must have seen her. Maybe you do not think you did. But if you saw a little girl on her own that day, ring the police. Try very hard.'

The family, who regularly spent weekends with the children's grandparents Terry, 58, and Lesley, 46, had spent that afternoon with Sarah playing on a beach with her brothers and sister. Mrs Payne was close to tears at an emotional press conference as it was explained how the adults returned to the house but allowed the four children, who knew the area well, to continue down the lane to play in the cornfield next to the property. 'Sarah is not the type to wander off on her own. The children always play together. They rely on each other. I do not understand this. She needs her family. We need her.'

Mrs Payne said that while they were playing 'dinosaurs', Sarah had wanted to go home shortly before 8pm. Mrs Payne, who has told her children they were not to blame for their sister's disappearance, said: 'Sarah got tired and just started walking off. Her brothers and sister were walking not even a minute behind her. Her brothers did not get to her in time. I don't understand how they weren't in sight of each other.' The nation was on tenterhooks as the heartbreaking hunt continued. Every day without news seemed grimmer than the day before. Sarah's tearful grandfather Terry then joined in the appeal for anyone who knew of her whereabouts. In two emotional letters read out by him at a press conference, the missing girl's siblings spoke of their pain. The granddad first read Charlotte's letter, decorated with pink hearts and kisses, in which she said: 'Please let her go because I love her, I love her, I love her. And please give her a rose and I will give her loads of kisses because I love her so much. When we bring her back I will give her something special. I love, I love, I love you so much I love you Sarah, Charlotte'.

Gripping the hand of the children's grandmother, Lesley, Mr Payne then read out the other letter written by Lee. 'To Sarah. If you're reading this please come home. We all miss you and want you back quick. We'll find you no matter what. We have a surprise for you when you come home. If anyone has got her let her go. We need her back we can't cope without her! We'll be looking forward to seeing her again. You are a little princess in the eyes of everyone and we'll always love you no matter what.' It was signed, 'Love you lots, Lee, Luke, Charlotte, Mum and Dad'.

Mr Payne added: 'If there is anybody out there who knows anything please ring us. It is tearing our family apart. Somebody has got Sarah. We really want her back, we love her so much. We are a very tight family, we just can't be without her. Please whoever is out there, somebody who knows something, please ring.'

Less than two weeks after her disappearance, an astonishing 12,000 calls had been received by police from people all over Britain who wanted to help find the girl. The police revealed they feared she might be hidden in the undergrowth of the countryside near where she was last seen. Sussex Police appealed to farmers, gamekeepers, forest rangers, wardens, walkers, utility workers, country cottage owners and anyone else familiar with the woods and fields between Crawley and the coast at Littlehampton to join them in the search. Superintendent Phil Clarke, in charge of the search teams, said: 'It seems to me that wherever Sarah is at the moment, she is very well hidden. There is an intention on the part of the people or the person hiding her that she should not be found.' He also said he hadn't given up hope that Sarah was alive but clearly the police knew they might be looking for a body.

The man in overall charge of the hunt, Sussex Assistant Chief Constable Nigel Yeo, also said he refused to give up hope that Sarah was alive and said his officers were not despondent. 'If anyone saw a van being worked on, in particular having its wooden panelling removed from the rear compartment or work on its doors, we want them to contact us,' he said. 'Such activity in Littlehampton or Worthing or the area just to the north would be of particular interest.'

The hunt came to its awful, yet predictable, end on 17 July. Farm labourer Luke Coleman was working in a field near Pulborough, ten miles from Sarah's home and 15 miles from where she disappeared, when he came across the naked body of a young girl. It was Sarah Payne. She was partially buried and the condition of the body made it impossible to establish the cause of death or whether the child had been sexually assaulted. It was thought likely she suffocated and her nakedness strongly suggested a sex offence. In the following weeks, 5,000 people left floral tributes near the site of her lonely grave alongside the A29.

The discovery prompted more headlines and a woman motorist, Mrs Deborah Bray, remembered seeing a child's sandal on a lane near the village of Coolham less than four miles from where her body was found. The shoe belonged to Sarah. It was the only item of her clothing that was ever recovered and it was to be a key piece of evidence in the case that the prosecution were eventually to present against Whiting. Exactly how it came to be there is a mystery that has not been solved. One possibility is that Whiting buried her clothes but forgot the shoe and then threw it away in panic.

After Whiting's arrest had become known, he had moved to his father's home in Crawley but it was attacked by a mob of about 30 stone-throwing youths and he had to escape. He began to sleep rough in the days that followed the discovery of Sarah's body and on 22 July he stole a Vauxhall Nova. But the police were watching him and gave chase.

Three times a pursuing police Volvo lost Whiting as he used his intimate knowledge of Crawley's side streets and his skills as a banger-car racer. He drove down lanes, across fields and playgrounds, through supermarket car parks, up ramps and even the wrong way along the busy A29. Twice he drove flat out at police cars. He drove through metal barriers, across central reservations and flattened bushes. Officers in the Volvo had to give up the chase because of damage to their car but the stolen car was driven to destruction: the chase ended when Whiting collided with a parked car.

There was no doubt that Whiting was chief suspect in the hunt for the killer and after he had appeared in a preliminary court hearing at Crawley charged with theft of a vehicle, assault and aggravated vehicle-taking, he was arrested for a second time in connection with Sarah and led from the court, his head covered by a blanket. A police spokesman said: 'A man aged in his forties and formerly from Littlehampton was arrested in Crawley and taken to an undisclosed police station for further questioning involving the murder of Sarah Payne. I can confirm that this was the same man who was arrested on Sunday 2 July regarding the suspected abduction of Sarah and was subsequently released on police bail pending further inquiries'.

Detective Superintendent Peter Kennet said: 'There is fresh evidence that is being followed up, but I couldn't go into the ins and outs of it'. He said police – who then had 96 hours to question Whiting before charging or releasing him – would not confirm the name of the arrested man. Mr Kennet added: 'Just because someone's arrested it doesn't mean to say that they will be charged.'

Even as he was being questioned, Whiting's ex-wife was being told of his arrest and saying: 'To say the least, I'm in shock at this happening. I have not seen him since Christmas 1995, when he brought a present round for our son. I have absolutely no feelings for him now whatsoever. But it still does take the wind out of your sails. We were going through a bad patch because his business wasn't bringing in money. That was the only thing wrong with the marriage: he did not have the money to support us.

'I was the only one bringing in a regular wage and we were always having arguments about it. There was never any chance of us getting back together – there was too much water under the bridge. I didn't even know where he was living. He had a girlfriend after me – she looked like a gangster's moll. She was only in her late teens or early twenties, quite a lot younger than him.'

At the end of August, Whiting's solicitor Gill McGivern spoke for him when he was taken from custody to appear before Crawley magistrates over the motoring matter. 'When Roy Whiting was arrested on suspicion of murder and interviewed, there were no legal grounds to either arrest or detain him,' she said. 'An application was made before the divisional court for a writ of habeas corpus and as a result of that he was bailed by police.'

Jail still beckoned for Whiting, however, because of the motoring offences, and he was sentenced to 22 months imprisonment at Chichester Crown Court at the end of September.

Months passed as the police and forensic officers' work continued unabated. At Christmas 2000 crucial forensic evidence began to emerge and Detective Superintendent Kennett received the text message: 'Call the scientists.'

'There was plenty of circumstantial evidence that he had killed Sarah,' he said later, 'but it wasn't until December that we got our first bit of real evidence. I was at the George & Dragon pub at Burpham, near Arundel, in West Sussex. I'd taken Mike and Sara Payne for a Christmas lunch. During the turkey and sprouts they were holding up better than me. Then I was paged to call a forensic scientist called Ray Chapman. To say I was excited is an understatement. "I think we might have something," he said to me.

'He went on to explain that among the hundreds of fibres on a Velcro strip on Sarah's shoe were four microscopic red fibres. They were identical to the red fibres of a sweatshirt recovered from the front of Whiting's Fiat Ducato van. There was also a blue fibre they were testing. It was the beginning of the end. Days later we got a result from the blue fibre. It had also been found on Sarah's shoe and, it turned out, matched fibres from a clown-pattern curtain in Whiting's van.'

He passed the news on to the Paynes. 'There was total silence around the table while I slowly told them, then a sigh of relief all round,' he recalled later.

The final piece of evidence, Mr Kennett said, slotted into place on the night of the police's own Christmas do, which was held in January because of the pressure of work. 'I'd popped home from the office to get changed when I got a phone call from the lead scenes-of-crime officer. On the red sweatshirt in Whiting's van had been 24 hairs, 23 of which gave no DNA profile whatsoever. But the last one did. The chances of it not being a strand of Sarah's hair were a billion to one. Roy Whiting had abducted and killed Sarah Payne.

'I met the Crown Prosecution Service in February and jokily told them that if they didn't take on the case, I'd arrest them for conspiracy to pervert the course of justice!'

So it was that by the beginning of February 2001, with Whiting still behind bars, stories began to appear in several newspapers referring to a 'vital breakthrough' in the case and suggesting an arrest might be imminent. Sure enough, on 6

February Whiting was arrested at 9.17am and driven to Bognor Regis police station, West Sussex, for questioning – the third time he had been arrested over her death.

Six hours later Detective Superintendent Kennett, flanked by Detective Superintendent Alan Ladley and Detective Inspector Martin Underhill, said outside the station: 'At 3.20pm today Roy William Whiting was charged with the murder of Sarah Payne.' He added: 'He was also additionally charged with the kidnap of Sarah. He will be appearing at Chichester Magistrates Court at 10am tomorrow. Sarah's parents Sara and Michael, of Hersham, Surrey, have been informed of the murder charge against Whiting.'

An angry crowd of more than 200 people gathered outside the court the next day. Some of them shouted 'Scum!' while others shouted 'Die!' and threw eggs at the car taking Whiting from court. The car, followed by two police vehicles, stopped 100 yards away at a level crossing and the crowd gave chase, but it sped away before they could reach it. Police blocked the road with a van to stop motorists chasing it, while up to 50 officers on foot spread out to block the crowd. One man was arrested on suspicion of causing criminal damage after he threw a drinks carton at the vehicle carrying Whiting. Another member of the public was arrested for a suspected public order offence.

On 19 February, at Lewes Crown Court, Sarah's parents saw for the first time the man accused of killing their daughter. Accompanied by Mike's parents, Terry and Lesley, the grieving couple were wearing badges bearing a picture of their little princess. Clasping each other's hands in a packed public gallery, they stared intently at the former mechanic during the seven-minute preliminary hearing before a judge.

Wearing a scruffy grey T-shirt and black jeans, and flanked by two security guards, Whiting – who had arrived in a three-van convoy surrounded by six motorbike riders – listened to proceedings, at one stage yawning, but didn't look up at the couple. His solicitor, Ms McGivern, said: 'It is anticipated that not guilty pleas will be entered in due course'. She added that the defence case would take several months to prepare and told the packed court: 'It is anticipated that the defence will not be ready until the end of this year, in November or December.'

When Whiting appeared in court again in May he entered 'not guilty' pleas to the murder and kidnapping charges, the first time he had publicly said anything about the crimes. This time Sara Payne was just a few feet away from the killer. Her husband was not in court – he found it too distressing.

The first trial of Roy Whiting was stopped after a few days for 'procedural reasons', but eventually it got underway at Lewes Crown Court in November 2001. Sussex Police had spent £2 million collecting the evidence they hoped would convict Whiting. The bill for forensic tests on 500 pieces of evidence alone came to £350,000. Officers on the murder squad had taken 2,300 written statements and searched 1,030 addresses; more than 4,000 photos had been taken and filed, and searches carried out along 70 miles of roads. A total of 1,022 police personnel had been involved.

Forensic evidence – especially DNA – was to prove vital among the evidence that the nine-man, three-woman jury heard. Twenty lever-arch files had been filled with hundreds of pages of notes by the team from the Forensic Science Service laboratory in London, and Raymond Chapman, who led the 18-month forensic investigation, told the jury about the evidence examined by his team.

Mr Chapman said Sarah's body was initially examined to see if any traces of Whiting's DNA could be found from blood or hair. Then Sarah's shoe was examined for fibres and more than 350 were found in its velcro strap. These were compared with fibres found on items from the cab of Whiting's white van, seized by police on the day of his arrest. Mr Chapman confirmed that among the 350 fibres checked, four were found that matched threads from a red sweatshirt which had been lying in the van. He also said one fibre from a clown-pattern curtain had been found in the van.

The court heard how the material was subject to a sequence of stringent chemical and physical examinations after being compared under a high-powered microscope. Matching fibres were then subject to microspectro-photometry, in which a beam of light is shone through the fibre and a computer detects how much light of each colour is absorbed. In the final test, dye was extracted from the fibre and separated into its constituent ingredients to analyse how it was manufactured.

Mr Chapman, one of the country's leading DNA and fibre experts, told the court the thread from the clown curtain was important because it was 'particularly distinctive'. He said: 'It starts off with a green colour then it becomes almost colourless. It starts to darken up and you have got a shade of grey or blue turning to black. It has also got a pink tinge to it. The vast majority of fibres are of one colour but with the curtain the colour has been printed on.'

A solitary blonde hair matching the full DNA profile of Sarah was also discovered on the red sweatshirt in Whiting's van. The prosecutor, Timothy Langdale, QC, asked Mr Chapman: 'If that hair, the hair found on the sweatshirt with the full profile matching Sarah Payne's DNA, if that hair did not come from Sarah Payne then the DNA profile must have been matched by chance?'

Mr Chapman replied: 'The chance of obtaining the match if that hair had come from somebody else would be in the order of one in one billion.'

Mr Chapman also told the court that a full DNA profile of Whiting had been obtained from the sweatshirt's cuffs and collar. Speaking of the testing of the collar and cuff, he said it was common if the police wished to find out if a person had worn that article of clothing. 'The police were interested in trying to show whether or not Mr Whiting had worn the sweatshirt. It's a fairly common thing to do. In some crimes an item of clothing is left behind and it's fairly common to extract the collar and cuff to try and get the DNA profile of the wearer.'

Other items of clothing found in Whiting's van had also yielded evidence. A partial DNA profile of Whiting – from a saliva stain – had been found on socks. Mr Chapman said the chance of obtaining that match if the DNA did not belong to

Whiting was one in 200,000. Semen found on the sleeve of a tartan sweatshirt also partially matched Whiting's DNA; the chances that it did not come from him were 6,800 to one. Five hairs from a green-checked shirt had been tested but no DNA profile could be found. Finally, a saliva stain on the clown-patterned curtain found in Whiting's van also matched the suspect's DNA profile.

If anything could make the trial more poignant, it came with Mr. Chapman's statement that Sarah's DNA had been obtained from a tooth of hers that the family had retained after she left it under her pillow for 'the tooth fairy'. She had left it there the night before she disappeared.

Sally O'Neill, QC, defending, urged the jury to totally disregard the evidence of Sarah's strand of hair. She said the sweatshirt could have been contaminated when it was sent to the forensic labs in the same van as two hairbrushes from the Paynes' home.

More touching evidence was heard by the jury when Sarah's brothers told, in video interviews, what had happened that summer's day. Lee described how the children were left playing in rock pools on the beach near their grandparents' house. He said Sarah had cried – but was 'always crying'. The boys had been told not to let Sarah out of their sight and Lee said: 'She was halfway across the field. Luke ran after her and stopped her.'

But Luke then began running back towards Lee. 'I don't know why Luke didn't stay with her.' Lee had then tried to catch her up. 'I was three quarters of the way across the field when I turned round to see where the others were.' When he turned back again his sister had gone. While he was still in the field, Lee said, he saw a white van driving along the lane at the edge of the field. When he got on to the lane, he saw what he believed was the same van driving past. He thought the van looked 'suspicious'. The driver grinned and waved. Lee said the man was scruffy as if he had been 'walking through bushes' and had 'yellowish teeth'. When Lee got back to his grandparents' house he asked his grandmother, Lesley, if his sister was there. She told him no and he said: 'I've lost her'. The boy said he did not feel responsible for his sister being missing but added: 'I feel as if I should have done something.'

Luke then said: 'I ran as fast as I could' to catch Sarah up. He was surprised at how quick she had been – she was normally a 'dawdler'. He added: 'I was ten seconds from catching up to Sarah.' He said he had run back to look after his other sister, Charlotte, five, who had been stung by a nettle. Lee had not been able to catch her, said Luke, because he was hampered by the corn, which came up to his waist. Luke remarked about the driver, 'We thought he might be out to get children'.

In an even more emotional moment, during Sara Payne's evidence, she gave a faint smile of recognition when asked to identify the silver puffa jacket given to her daughter as a gift. She had been handed the garment as prosecutor Mr Langdale asked: 'Look at this coat – do you recognise it?' Sara managed to reply: 'Yes. Sarah got that for Christmas from her grandparents.

'I don't think she wore it on the day. It was very warm. It was her favourite coat because it was much more adult than her others. It was her first adult coat with sleeves you could detach.'

Then she hugged the youngster's blue school sweatshirt with the badge of Bell Farm Primary on the front. It was the first time in months that Sara had been close to either piece of clothing because both had been taken away as evidence. Mr Langdale had earlier told the court that blue fibres taken from the lining of the coat were linked to a sweatshirt worn by her killer.

As for Sarah's shoe, Mr Payne managed a small smile as she said that because her daughter loved wearing shoes rather than trainers, and as she was 'heavy on her feet' they were already worn down.

When asked by Mr Langdale about the baby tooth that scientists had used to obtain a DNA profile of the youngster, she said: 'It came out on the Friday night. She put it under her pillow for when she got back after the weekend.'

Recalling the night Sarah vanished, her mother said of the four playing children: 'They asked if they could stay on the beach and as it was such a lovely evening we decided that they could. My last words to them were, "Please stay together". As we were walking along, I looked back and they were playing on the beach.'

Soon afterwards the children left the beach, walked past the house in Peak Lane where their grandmother Lesley was waiting and went into a cornfield. She said the adults had dropped in at a pub and bought wine and cigarettes before heading home. 'As we left the pub the Lottery show was just coming on the TV. We walked around the estate and when we got to Peak Lane, Les was standing right down at the bottom, which was quite unusual.

'I was trying to look and see if she [Sarah] had fallen because it wasn't like her [to disappear]. We all looked backwards and forwards. We searched some places twice. We were always coming home to check with Lesley to see if she had come back. Then we went out in the car. We went back to the house, I think it was about 9pm, and we had been looking for an hour. We decided it was time to call the police.'

Even the courage of Sarah's parents reached breaking point, however, as they left the court separately after hearing the terrible details of the discovery of her body.

Pathologist Vesna Djurovic told the jury that Sarah met a 'violent death' and added that she believed the youngster was the victim of a 'sexually motivated homicide'.

Jurors stopped taking notes and looked shaken as she told how decomposition had made it impossible to say for sure if Sarah had suffered any internal or external injuries. There was no pathological evidence to show sexual assault but it could not be excluded. Dr Djurovic was unable to give an exact cause of death but believed Sarah was asphyxiated.

A statement from farm labourer Luke Coleman described how he was clearing ragwort from a field on the edge of a main road when he approached what he thought was a dead animal. 'I saw what I thought to be a dead deer. It was about seven feet away from the road. As I approached I could see it was not a deer, but the body of a child. I could see a leg with a foot pointing diagonally upwards and I could see it was naked. I was so shocked that I could not remember if it was face down or on its side.'

One element of the case was the attempts Whiting made to get rid of the traces of Sarah's short stay in his van. Giving evidence, Mr Terry Heath, who had employed him as a labourer, said Whiting always looked scruffy and dirty on building sites. But he saw him the day after Sarah's disappearance outside his Littlehampton flat and he was 'very smart and very clean, steam cleaned'.

On day 13 of the trial, Whiting entered the witness box to give evidence, the first time in 17 months that he had spoken publicly of the events of that weekend. Wearing jeans and a burgundy sweatshirt, he sat hunched forward with his elbows on his knees for almost five hours under intense questioning. He spoke in a nasal, estuary-English monotone with a slight lisp as he described what he claimed to have been doing the day Sarah was snatched, admitting that he had visited three parks and a funfair, gone for a long walk on a beach and visited a boating lake on the coast. But he insisted it was 'pure chance' that he went to places where children would be and denied that he had kitted out his van with a series of items that could be used in kidnapping, tying up and threatening children in the back.

He also told a court he had 'no answer' to why he didn't protest immediately that he was innocent of anything to do with Sarah's abduction and murder, even though he might have been able to provide a complete alibi after police arrested him the next day. From the moment he was arrested he had repeatedly 'stonewalled', the court was told, giving 'no comment' answers to key questions during 12 interviews spread over eight months.

His defence counsel, Sally O'Neill, QC, told him: 'You are charged with the kidnap and murder of Sarah Payne. Have you in any shape or form been associated with that young girl?'

Whiting: 'No.'

Miss O'Neill: 'Or had anything to do with her death?'

Whiting: 'Nothing whatsoever.'

Then Mr Langdale, prosecuting, asked Whiting why he had not simply told police about driving around the parks that Saturday evening?

Whiting replied he had been 'on auto-pilot' and 'in a daydream'.

Mr Langdale said: 'If there was an ounce of truth in that account, why not say that to the police? It would have taken you 15 seconds.'

Whiting replied: 'I don't know. Possibly they wouldn't believe me.'

Mr Langdale said: 'The reason is, you were in a bit of a difficulty trying to tell the police where you had been the previous evening.'

Whiting said: 'No.'

Mr Langdale: 'Because you had, in fact, been involved in the kidnap of this very little girl they had come to talk to you about. True?'

Whiting: 'Not true.'

Mr Langdale: 'That was the problem, wasn't it?'

Whiting: 'No.'

Mr Langdale: 'You were trying to conceal from the police not only what you were doing on the Saturday but also on the Sunday. That's where you were having trouble. You had not worked out your story.'

Whiting: 'I had no story to work out.'

Mr Langdale: 'The reason you were not telling them the truth as an innocent man was that you were a guilty man.'

Whiting: 'That's not true.'

Mr Langdale also suggested that if Whiting had been innocent, the petrol receipt could have provided the perfect alibi to prove he had nothing to do with Sarah's killing. He told him: 'You must have thought "Goodness gracious me, that proves where I was." You told us as an innocent man that you had nothing to do with Sarah Payne's abduction, and that you had not the slightest idea that Sarah Payne's body was buried rather nearer to the Buck Barn garage than to Littlehampton. Police were still trying to find that little girl. Being able to prove that you were at the garage shortly before 10 o'clock might have been the complete alibi for you in relation to her disappearance. Then why did you not just say so to the police?'

Whiting said: 'The solicitor advised me to make no comment. It was hard for me to sit there and not answer the questions.'

Mr Langdale: 'But there was something that could prove you had nothing to do with Sarah's disappearance. So you could have said: "There you are, Mr Policeman. That proves where I was – I could not have been involved." Then why not make that point to the police?'

Whiting: 'I have no answer to that.'

Mr Langdale: 'You have no answer to that because the real reason you were not going to say anything about the Buck Barn garage receipt was because you were the only person then who knew where Sarah Payne's body was buried. That's the real reason, isn't it?'

Whiting: 'No.'

The QC then pointed out that Whiting had never asked police when and where Sarah disappeared. He added: 'I'm making the point to you that you never asked them what time she disappeared. That's another pointer to the fact that you are guilty because you didn't need to ask you knew.'

Whiting denied lying about his movements. He said that when he told police he had 'not gone out' of his Littlehampton flat on Sunday, he meant he had 'not gone out of the town'.

Whiting was also accused of lying about the reason and the timing of removing the plywood panelling from the back of his van and changing the rear doors. He said for the first time that he had dumped the wood at a local tip and then denied the QC's suggestion that he had 'never said a word' about it because he didn't want police to find the wood.

'The reason you were worried about that was because Sarah Payne had been in the back of your van, hadn't she?'

Whiting: 'No.'

Whiting also said it was 'pure chance' that the places he had visited on Saturday afternoon and evening were places where young children might be.

The QC asked: 'Why were you going to places like that?

Because the suggestion is that the man who abducted Sarah, and you know I'm suggesting that was you, was someone who was out on the prowl looking for a child.'

Whiting denied this but admitted that he didn't go on any rides at the funfair.

He was then questioned about a series of photographs of items which were found in the back of his van. There was a rope, which he knew about, but he claimed a set of plastic ties, looped together in a figure of eight, did not belong to him. A knife in the van was used for stripping wire, he said. The bottle of Johnson's baby oil was to relieve dry hands from building work.

He added he had never been to Coolham, where Sarah's shoe was discovered, and denied that he had used a spade found in the back of the van to bury Sarah's little blue dress. Mud on his jeans, sweatshirt and trainers was not from burying anything.

Mr Langdale: 'You were responsible for her body being in that field.' Whiting: 'No, I was not responsible.'

The next day Whiting continued to give evidence. At one stage Mr Langdale interrupted one of his answers and said: 'You're just making this up as you go along, aren't you?'

Mr Langdale also questioned him on the 22 tiny fibres, which he said associated Whiting with Sarah. The discovery of the fibres, he said, was revealed to Whiting during his third police interview on 6 February. 'You must have been appalled to discover that you, an entirely innocent man, had got a problem with fibres linking you to the death of this little girl. The game was up, wasn't it?'

Whiting: 'No.' He added that he had given no explanation for them purely on the advice of his lawyer, who told him to make no comment.

One fibre 'indistinguishable' from those in the curtain was found on the Velcro strap of Sarah's little black shoe. Asked if this was just a coincidence Whiting shrugged his shoulders.

The prosecutor then asked: 'Was it also coincidence that four other fibres indistinguishable from his red sweatshirt were found on the same shoe?'

Whiting: 'It's a very common sweatshirt.'

Four more fibres were found in Sarah's hair.

Whiting: 'As I say, it's a very common sweatshirt.'

Other fibres from articles in his van were found in the bag that police used to remove Sarah's body. Some from his socks were found in her hair. 'They're common socks – I've got four pairs.'

Mr Langdale asked: 'So it's a whole series of unfortunate coincidences?' Whiting: 'Yes.'

As for the single blonde hair from Sarah which was found on Whiting's red sweatshirt, that too he said, was a coincidence.

But that strand of hair, and the DNA evidence that it belonged to Sarah, was a vital piece of the jigsaw of evidence that the jury considered for nine hours before returning their verdict – guilty on both charges.

Calls for 'Sarah's Law' – increased public knowledge of the whereabouts movements of sex offenders – reached a crescendo with the verdict and the knowledge, which at last became public, of his earlier sex offence against the young girl. The jury had not been told of it during the trial and as they listened to the details of it, the young forewoman of the jury burst into tears and another woman juror held her head in her hands.

Whiting listened without any sign of emotion as Mr Justice Curtis sentenced him to life and – in a rare move in an English court – said he should never be released. He would die behind bars. The judge summed up his own, and the nation's mood, when he told Whiting he had kidnapped Sarah to fulfil his 'abnormal sexual desires'. He described as 'ludicrous' Whiting's claim that he bought his white van for his job as a mechanic and builder. The judge then detailed the various implements that Whiting had in the van – including a knife, rope, cushion, baby oil and the plastic ties looped like handcuffs – and added: 'I am quite satisfied that you indecently assaulted her in it. One of the many articles had a small trace of semen on it.'

'As we all know,' the judged added, 'you stripped Sarah naked and you suffocated her and buried her and got rid of her clothes – you are indeed an evil man. What is more you did the same thing in early 1995, but that girl you mercifully did not kill. The medical evidence shows that you are in no way mentally unwell. I have seen you for a month or so and heard you give evidence and I believe you are a cunning and glib liar.'

He then referred to a psychiatric report produced after the first attack that had described him as a 'high risk' repeat offender. 'How right he was,' observed the judge. He said that Whiting had claimed to police when first quizzed over Sarah's disappearance that he had "learned his lesson" from his previous offence. He said: 'Nothing could be further from the truth.' Describing the murder as 'truly appalling', he added: 'You are every parent's and every grandparent's nightmare come true. My judgement is that you are and will remain an absolute menace to any little girl. It's one of the rare cases where I shall recommend to the appropriate authorities that you be kept in prison for the rest of your life so that no further child is added to the list of your victims and the lives of a third family are not ruined.'

He ended with the words: 'You may go down.'

As Whiting turned to descend the stone steps, Sarah's grandfather, Terry, spat at him and shouted: 'I hope you rot!'

5

THE ANGLESEY VAMPIRE

The story in *The Liverpool Post* of an elderly woman's death one day in November 2001 seemed like yet another sad comment on life in modern Britain. It read: 'Police launched a major investigation in North Wales last night after the suspicious death of an elderly woman. Neighbours were shocked after the grim discovery of Mabel Leyshon's body at her home in Llanfairpwll, Anglesey. Detective Chief Inspector John Clayton, leading the investigation, said: "Police were called to the house where the body of an elderly woman was found. We are treating the death as suspicious at the present time and a major investigation is being launched."

'Mr Clayton added: "It is too early at this stage to go into detail but the investigation has been launched because of the way the body was found and all lines of inquiry will be followed up."'

Most readers probably assumed it was yet another case of an elderly person being attacked by a burglar in the so-called safety of their own home, no longer the shocking news that it once was in Britain. As the facts began to emerge, however, Mr Clayton's use of the word 'suspicious' seemed one of the most understated summaries of a crime ever made.

Obviously his words were carefully chosen for operational reasons, but the truth was that he and his colleagues were dealing with one of the most gory, perverted slayings in recent criminal history. For frail, deaf, 90-year-old Mabel, who also suffered from poor eyesight, was the victim of a 'vampire' who had cut out her heart, drained the blood from her body into a saucepan and then drunk it.

Mabel, who was just 4ft 9in tall, had been widowed for over 40 years and lived alone at her bungalow home in Lin Pant, Llanfairpwll, overlooking the Menai Straits. She was found dead by police in her living room after a meals-on-wheels woman couldn't get a reply. The visitor saw that a patio door at the rear of the house had been smashed, so she called the police. The officers who arrived made the grim discovery of the body, which had been repeatedly stabbed.

Detective Chief Inspector Clayton revealed a little more of the true horror inside her home when, a few days later, he said: 'The injuries are probably the worst that I have seen in my career and it is very important that we catch this person as soon as we possibly can. The offender may be bloodstained so I would appeal to anyone who has a relative, friend or associate who has, since Friday, come home bloodstained or with bloodstained clothing to contact the police and we will carry out enquiries about that person. If anyone has any information at all about callers to the house, any visitors, any workers, anybody at all, please contact us.'

As forensic officers busied themselves at the scene, Mr Clayton said that police had established the cause of death as multiple stab wounds, but there was no clear time of death. 'It isn't an exact science but we believe that there is a strong possibility that Mrs Leyshon died sometime late Saturday or early Sunday.'

'I would say, at this stage, that there is nothing obvious in the house that has been disturbed. We are carrying out a slow and very detailed forensic examination of the scene and when that is finished we will need to get people who know what is in the house to carry out a full inventory. The point of entry at the rear of the house is what I would describe as a typical burglary – a smashed window at the base of a patio door. There is no obvious sign of a search by an intruder.

'We haven't found a weapon but all we can say at this stage is that it is a bladed weapon. There are no obvious signs of a struggle but there are multiple stab wounds to the lady's hands and body.'

Mr Clayton declined to give details of the exact nature of the wounds suffered by Mrs Leyshon, but a strong clue soon emerged when those officers – who said they had never encountered such savagery – turned to law enforcement agencies with experience of similar crimes. 'We will be liaising with the FBI in America and all forces in this country,' Mr Clayton said. 'It is so rare we have to look at the experience of others who have been involved in investigating these sorts of crimes.'

Britain's National Crime Faculty and a criminal psychologist – a Cracker-style figure – had already been enlisted to create a profile of the maniac. And madman he must have been, for three weeks after her death, police at last revealed the full extent of the slaying. Mabel's heart had been cut out from her body and then placed in a saucepan on a nearby silver platter. Two brass pokers had also been placed alongside her body in the form of a cross.

On the eve of the murder featuring on BBC's *Crimewatch*, one of the senior officers involved, Detective Superintendent Alan Jones, said: 'It is important that the public understand the type of individual we are looking for. That individual actually removed Mabel Leyshon's heart.'

The police were looking at theories that the killer might have had some form of medical training to carry out such an attack and began to interview butchers and abattoir workers, men who might be able to carry out such a gruesome task. But the publicity the case attracted and the *Crimewatch* item played a key part in tracking down the killer, because they brought to light a previous 'vampire' incident involving the young man who was to be charged with Mabel's murder.

As Christmas and New Year came and went, the pervading fear on the close-knit community of Anglesey was that the monster would strike again. That terror only came to an end when, in January, 17-year-old Mathew Hardman was arrested and charged with Mabel's murder.

Hardman was not named at the time of arrest nor, indeed, when his trial began that summer at Mold Crown Court, sitting in the nearby city of Chester. It was only then that the full details of Mabel's gruesome death emerged. The court was told that Hardman had committed the 'sacrifice' after having read about how to become a vampire and attain immortality.

Prosecutor Roger Thomas, QC, said: 'He may now deny it or seek to play it down but we submit that in November 2001 he was fascinated by and believed in vampires. He believed they existed, believed they drank human blood and believed most importantly that they could achieve immortality – and he wanted to be immortal.

What may have started out as a bizarre interest became an obsession and led ultimately to murder.'

Wearing gloves, Hardman – 6ft 2in tall and muscular from working out regularly – had broken into little Mrs Leyshon's house while the pensioner watched television, no doubt turned up loud so she could hear it – in her lounge. He then attacked her from behind, stabbing her 22 times, including one wound that was so deep he was able to tear out her heart. He then took off most of Mrs Leyshon's clothes and put her body in an armchair with her legs propped up on a stool, before draining her blood into a small saucepan.

'This is an incident that a person has taken some time over and possibly enjoyed, because the blood in the saucepan has dried out before the newspaper [with the heart inside it] is put into it,' said Mr Thomas.

'By 24 November 2001, the defendant had learned quite a

lot about vampires, certainly enough to satisfy his two main questions: how do I become a vampire and how do I become immortal? He had decided what he had to do – a sacrifice. The murder of another human being was necessary to achieve his ends. And with his parents away he committed what we submit to you was a planned, deliberate murder to satisfy his own grotesque and selfish ends.'

The youth was not insane, he added, but carried out the murder because of his obsession with vampires.

Detective Constable Kevin John Howell was the first CID officer to arrive at the bungalow at Llanfairpwll. He told the court how when he entered the lounge, he saw the pokers in an apparent cross in front of the fireplace, a silver candlestick on the floor which had blood on it, a red candle on the mantelpiece and a saucepan containing newspaper next to the chair where the body was.

After a doctor had formally certified death, the officer said that he had placed a travel rug over the body. Shortly afterwards, he and other policemen had conducted a search inside and outside the house, as well as the garage.

A key part of the evidence was Hardman's DNA profile which put him at the murder scene. The 'vampire' had drained her blood into the saucepan before drinking it and as result of this action a lip-mark was found on it. Forensic scientist Jacqueline Gardener said that the defendant's DNA was also found at the point of entry into her bungalow and that the chances of the DNA profile being that of someone else was one in 73 million.

Regarding the DNA profile, Miss Gardener said that marks

found at the window of Mrs Leyshon's home had been made by an item wet with blood coming into contact with the surface. Heavily bloodstained clothing with a number of stab holes were also found in her home.

Among the other evidence was a footprint found at the scene from an unusual Levi's trainer, which matched a pair owned by the teenager and, crucially, a knife was found in his possession that had a partial DNA profile matching the widow's.

The jury also heard how, some two months before the murder, Hardman had gone to the lodgings of a 16-year-old German girl student called Anna Hassler, whom he had met through a friend, 18-year-old Chinese student David Lam, who lived in the same lodgings. He had chatted to her for over two hours before accusing her of being a vampire and begging her to transform him into one by biting his neck. When Anna refused he became violent and the police were called.

Lam told the court that on that night, Hardman had visited him at his lodgings and started talking about things he did not understand. Hardman then went to the bedroom of the German student who was staying there, to talk to her. Lam heard the girl shouting: 'Don't, don't, don't!' but thought that his friend was chatting her up and so did nothing.

When the householder returned later the girl student called out to her, and she ran into the bedroom. Lam followed and saw Hardman, who appeared 'crazy' and was shouting the girl's name. 'He said something about her being a vampire and she looked scared,' he said. 'I tried to stop him and slapped his face once,' he said. The slap had no effect. Hardman kept asking the girl student to bite him. The landlady was trying to stop him but she could not.

'I slapped him again and tried to get him out of the house. We could only manage to get him into the dining room. He was very strong. He was not scared of anyone,' said Lam.

Hardman then punched himself in the face, Lam continued, and his nose bled. 'He told me to smell his blood.'

Sergeant Peter Nicholson told the court that he went to the house in the early hours of Sunday, 23 September. 'Inside the house I saw a male youth sitting on a settee. I attempted to speak to him to try to get him to leave peacefully. He didn't make any sort of coherent response. All he could say was: "Bite my neck".'

Hardman was handcuffed and arrested for breach of the peace before being taken to the local police station, but he was never charged with any offence.

The court was also told that Hardman, a regular user of cannabis, had a love of the macabre and that he would paint gruesome pictures showing people being decapitated or disembowelled. His favourite artist was the controversial Mexican Frida Kahlo, famed for her self-portraits which often expressed her great physical pain and suffering through almost surreal symbolism.

The police later found that Hardman had spent hours on the Internet, logging on to sites such as The Vampire Rights Movement and The Vampire/Donor Alliance. That site claimed: 'The site exists to serve all who might be part of vampire community: gothic lifestyle vampires and non-lifestyle vampires alike, energy feeders, sanguinarians (drinkers of blood); donors, would-be donors, and other loved ones.' They also found two copies of the 'alternative' magazine *Bizarre*, featuring articles on how to cook and eat human flesh and how to perform a black mass.

Some weeks prior to the murder, Hardman had also asked friends how he could go about becoming a vampire. He'd said the village was a perfect place for vampires because it was full of old people and if they were bitten and died, everyone would blame a heart attack.

When Detective Constable Dewi Harding Jones arrested Hardman on 8 January 2002 at his family home – a few minutes walk from the murder scene – he turned to his mother and said: 'Don't worry. It's all right, Mum. I didn't do anything.' When, after they charged him, the police asked if he wanted anything, he said: 'Yes, I'll have a Big Mac and fries.'

Hardman's defence was that he had only started carrying the knife for protection after the horrific murder occurred. He only had a 'subtle' interest in vampires, he said, and he had looked at books and internet sites including the Vampire Rights Movement out of interest.

The trial lasted three weeks but it took the jury just three and three quarter hours to reach a unanimous verdict of guilty. As the verdict was announced, Hardman's mother, Julia, screamed and cried from the public gallery. Sitting directly above him, she leaned over the court railings with her arms stretched out to him and called out: 'I love you, son.'

Mr Justice Richards, who finally allowed Hardman's name to be made public after the verdict was announced, described the murder as an act of great wickedness which had no explanation apart from his vampire obsession and said he had been convicted by the jury on the strength of most compelling evidence.

'The horrific nature of this murder is plain to all. It was a vicious, sustained attack on an elderly lady in her own home... It was planned and carefully calculated.

Why you, an otherwise pleasant and otherwise well-regarded young man should act in this way is difficult to comprehend. But I am driven to the conclusion on the evidence I have heard that vampirism had become a near-obsession with you – that you really did believe that the myth might be true, that you thought you might in some way achieve immortality by drinking another person's blood and that you found this an irresistible attraction.

'One might hope for a psychiatric explanation for your behaviour,' the judge added, but there was no mental illness or disorder. Reports showed there might be some well-disguised underlying psychiatric illness which was not presently diagnosed, but 'I must proceed on the basis that you are of sound mind and must look for an explanation elsewhere.'

The judge said that even though he allowed for confusion and a degree of immaturity in Hardman and his childish fantasies, 'the fact remains that this was an act of great wickedness, one you have not faced up to or shown any remorse for... You had hoped for immortality. All you achieved was to brutally end another person's life and the bringing of a life sentence upon yourself.' He ordered that the 17-year-old should be detained at Her Majesty's Pleasure and ruled that he should serve a minimum of 12 years.

Shortly after he was jailed, his loyal mother visited him in jail to celebrate his 18th birthday. Mrs Hardman, a 50-year-old psychiatric nurse who was separated from the killer's father, said the vampire connection was introduced because forensic evidence was weak, and that DNA found at Mrs Leyshon's home resulted from her son delivering newspapers there for three years. 'He has emphatically said he did not do it and I believe him. I have always been adamant that he has not done it.

'When the jury gave the guilty verdict, I screamed because I could see Mathew was crying and his whole body was shaking.' And she added, as perhaps only a mother could: 'He was never one to get into a fight and he was very caring towards older people, like his grandparents.'

Detective Superintendent Jones, who had led the 50–strong investigating team, agreed that Hardman had shown no remorse or sympathy, but said he could not speculate about what might have been going on inside his head. 'The mutilation of the body is something we all had difficulty in trying to explain. To kill someone – you can find an explanation. But to attack someone already dead, there must be a reason for it. We struggled for some weeks to find out what that would be. When we found the lip-mark, perhaps the picture became clearer.'

6

MY TWIN'S THE RAPIST, NOT ME

Dan Brown's blockbuster novel *The Da Vinci Code* brought worldwide fame to Rosslyn Chapel, the 15th-century church in the village of Roslin, a few miles south of the Scottish capital, Edinburgh.

In the late spring of 2005, preparations were well underway for film stars Tom Hanks and Audrey Tatou to fly in for eight days of shooting the movie version of the book, in which the climax centres on dramatic events inside the church. The film's director, Ron Howard, had already mingled with tourists and worshippers after the deal to film there had been arranged with the chapel's trustees and the car park had to triple in size to make room for all the extra sightseers as visiting figures trebled to over 100,000 a year.

Even if they hadn't read the book or didn't plan to see the film, visitors would still be enchanted by the area, which is listed in guides to the best walks in Britain. One description reads: 'Tree-lined paths take you beside a river to a special ancient chapel in this glorious glen.'

One such sightseer on 15 May that year was a 19-year-old Dutch shop-worker. Shortly before 6 pm, she was walking through the nearby Roslin Glen Wildlife Centre en route to a friend's home in the nearby village of Rosewell, where she was planning to stay the night. The girl, who was wearing a light-pink chiffon dress over a multi-coloured, zigzag-patterned top, had been working in Edinburgh for some months and was strolling alongside the B7003 road when she suddenly became part of real-life events as dramatic as anything an author could imagine.

That chain of events began when a man approaching her in broad daylight suddenly pushed the teenager down the steep, 45ft roadside embankment. There he pinned her to the ground, savagely punched her in the face again and again, threatened her with a knife, asked if she was a virgin – she refused to answer – and then raped her. She screamed, shouted and struggled, but to no avail. His warped lust satisfied, the man then ran off, leaving his battered victim alone and traumatised. Eventually she managed to drag herself up the embankment and flag down a passing motorist.

The driver, a woman, at first thought the girl had been hit by a car, such were her terrible facial injuries. As she was rushed to Edinburgh Royal Infirmary, the forensic team moved in to examine the spot and the hunt began for her attacker.

Detective Superintendent Andy Waddell of Lothian and

Borders Police said police were eager to catch the rapist before he could strike again. 'It is a great concern that someone who could carry out such a violent and brutal attack is still at large. Although the attack took place in a rural setting, the nearby road is a through road between Penicuik and Bonnyrigg. We want anyone who thinks they may have seen someone suspicious around the area to get in touch.'

The rapist was described as white, in his thirties, 5ft 9-10ins tall, medium build, round face, pale complexion and cropped brown short hair with a fringe cut across the forehead. He was possibly wearing a light-coloured T-shirt tucked into blue denim jeans and distinctive yellow/tan rigger-style boots. Mr Waddell added: 'We are keen to hear from anyone who may have been walking or driving along the B7003 near Rosewell late yesterday afternoon and remembers seeing this man with his distinctive boots. This was a particularly serious sexual assault which has left a young woman injured and severely traumatised.'

The young victim, who was never identified as the attack she suffered was a sexual one, bravely gave detectives as much information as she could, including revisiting the spot of the attack. The police continued to appeal for information, saying: 'We have had reports of a man acting strangely around Bonnyrigg and are keen to trace him. Another man with a walking stick and a plastered leg chatted to the victim while she was at the chapel. We are keen to speak to him, as he may be able to provide us with help identifying the attacker.'

Detective Inspector Ronnie Millar, who was leading the

inquiry, said: 'The victim was quite distinctively dressed. We hope that by releasing details of what she was wearing more witnesses will come forward who might remember seeing her on the day. We would like to hear from anyone who may have been at Rosslyn Chapel on Sunday afternoon around 5pm and remembers seeing her, or anyone driving along the B7003 after that time and recalls her walking along the road.'

More than 250 motorists were interviewed as the hunt continued and police said: 'It is possible that the victim's attacker may have suffered scratches due to the heavy undergrowth near the scene of the assault. We don't believe the victim managed to scratch her attacker but he may have marks on his body. We appeal for anyone who knows someone who may not be able to explain some unusual marks to come forward.'

Two weeks later the appeals stopped. Instead came the announcement that the police had been longing to make when, on 27 May, a Lothian and Borders Police spokesman said: 'A 27-year-old man has been arrested and charged with a serious sexual assault in Rosewell on 15 May.' DNA traces on a discarded cannabis joint had led them to Robert Greens, a convicted criminal. Three days later at Edinburgh Sheriff Court, Greens, 27 and from Mayfield in Midlothian, was charged with assault to severe injury and rape. He was also charged with having a lock knife in a public place and having cannabis and cannabis resin. Greens made no plea or declaration and was remanded in custody as the case was continued for 'further examination'.

As the case against him was prepared, the kind-hearted

folk of the area raised more than £300 for the victim from collection jars in local shops and pubs, as well as the community's bowling club and churches. Linda McAra, barmaid at the Rosedale Arms pub, said: 'There was a collection jar put on the bar and some of the regulars put some money in. Everyone was shocked when they heard about the attack, which happened really close to the village. People just wanted to do something nice for the girl.' The cash was handed over to the victim's police liaison officer, who forwarded it on.

In a letter of thanks to the villagers, the girl wrote: 'For so many fellow humans to show their love and kindness to me is heart-warming, and helps to restore my trust in humankind.' It needed to be restored. When she first looked at her injuries in the mirror the poor girl was so horrified at what she saw that she then covered up all the mirrors in her home so that she would not catch a glimpse of herself.

Come October, as Tom Hanks was busy filming at Rosslyn Chapel, Greens was pleading not guilty at the High Court in Edinburgh to assaulting the 19-year-old 'to her severe injury and to the danger of her life' and raping her.

Then, on 26 October, came the astonishing development that made this case one of the most sensational ever to feature DNA evidence. At a pre-trial hearing at the High Court in Edinburgh, two special defences were lodged: one of alibi and one of incrimination. The alibi defence was simple: he was elsewhere when the attack took place. The incrimination was nothing short of historic, because Robert Greens was saying that the DNA that pointed to him being the attacker could in fact belong to Richard Greens – his identical twin brother.

Jane Farquharson, defending Greens, told the judge, Lord Abernethy: 'He says he was not there at the time. Another explanation for the DNA may be that it is his identical twin brother because twin brothers share the same DNA.' Ms Farquharson lodged the two special defences of alibi and incrimination and in them Robert Greens stated he was at a number of addresses in the Penicuik area, including a miners' welfare club, at the time of the attack, and that the student was attacked and raped by Richard Greens of Fort William – his identical twin.

Identical twins are the only type of people who share the same DNA make-up; for one twin to blame the other for such a serious crime meant the literature of crime would never be the same again.

But how can it be that two people have the same DNA fingerprint? The reason is simple: identical twins are formed when one fertilised egg in the mother splits in two, giving them DNA that cannot be told apart – unlike non-identical or 'fraternal' twins, where two different eggs are fertilised and there is only a 50 per cent similarity.

Fortunately for crime-fighters, identical twins can be told apart by their fingerprints, as in the first six to thirteen weeks of life inside the womb, the infant touches the mother's amniotic sack, resulting in changes to the fingerprints that remain for life.

Bearing all this in mind, defence lawyers had previously asked for more time to obtain a report by an expert witness on the crucial DNA evidence. The judge agreed to another preliminary hearing the next month with the trial – with the Dutch girl able to give evidence from behind a screen – unlikely to start before early 2006.

Shortly before Christmas 2005, this astonishing case took another unexpected turn when, after two months of frantic activity behind the scene, Robert Greens, by now shaven-headed, changed his plea at the second preliminary hearing at Edinburgh High Court and admitted raping the girl. His defence counsel, Donald Findlay, QC, told the court that Green was pleading guilty to rape, while advocate depute, Peter Hammond, asked the court for further time before delivering an account of the crime, so that arrangements could be made for anyone wishing to attend the proceedings. The judge, Lord Mackay of Drumadoon, agreed to continue the case until January and remanded Greens in custody.

The full story at last could be told. Robert Greens had begun his criminal career in his early teens and was sent to a residential school for young offenders. As a teenager he stole cars and broke into houses before receiving a two-year sentence in 1996 for assault and robbery. He was given another 30 months that August, again for assault and robbery. He then worked in a variety of casual jobs before joining a travelling fairground and moving around the country for a number of months.

In 2002, he had started work for William Sinclair Horticulture as a peat-cutter and moved to the Mayfield district, not far from Rosslyn Chapel, with his young family. This was about four months before the attack on the teenager. At the time of the outrage he had three daughters with his wife Angela, who were five, three and one. Indeed, his wife gave birth to a fourth child while he was in custody.

On that fateful day, before parking his car in the lay-by near where he attacked his victim, Greens had smoked 15 joints of super-strength 'skunk' cannabis and drunk ten pints of lager and cider at a number of pubs. He had even been smoking a joint when he grabbed her – it fell from his mouth but was later recovered by police. It was found to have traces of his DNA on it, as had some of the girl's clothing.

Detective Inspector Ronnie Millar was to say: 'Greens had been smoking a lot of 'skunk' on the day in question. He was working in the morning at a peat farm and went on a pub crawl with friends in Penicuik during the afternoon until 5pm, when he kept on smoking.'

He went on to describe what happened when Greens met the girl. 'Greens pushed her down a steep embankment and beat her very badly in the face. It was a horrendous attack. The woman who found her and the first police officer on the scene both thought she had been hit by a car. It wasn't until about ten minutes later when she was in the ambulance that she had calmed down enough to tell them she had been raped. Greens showed no remorse at all and lied through his teeth during the interviews. He was willing to hang his brother out to dry to get away with it. Greens had claimed that he had met with members of his family during the time of the attack. He had quite an extended family in Penicuik and they supported his alibis. It took a lot of work to establish that the timing was off and to prove them to be false.

'When we detained him outside his house two weeks after the incident, he was on his way to work. He had a couple of ounces of skunk in his pocket.'

Mr Millar paid tribute to the bravery of the victim who had been left traumatised by her ordeal. 'She has now begun her studies at university, but she suffers from a degree of agoraphobia and tends to stay inside. She's still struggling to cope. The ordeal has also hit her family hard. I understand her father has found it particularly difficult to deal with.'

Another who found it difficult to comprehend the magnitude of Greens' attack, albeit in a vastly different way, was his twin brother, Richard Greens, the father of three young sons. While the teenager was being brutalised in the beauty spot, Richard was at a barbecue more than 130 miles away in Fort William. He only learned that he was in the frame for the rape when police came to his home two weeks after the attack.

'They basically told us they knew it was Robert but because we are identical twins they had to speak to me too. It really disgusted me. They questioned me and took DNA and they said my brother had blamed me.'

But Richard and his wife had been enjoying their barbecue with pals in Fort William when the rape happened: 'We were there from about 2pm until 8pm. It was a great day, everyone had a drink. We knew nothing about what was happening in Midlothian.'

Despite his watertight alibi, Richard became the victim of

a hate campaign once the possibility that he might be the rapist became public. His home was attacked and the stress led to him taking anti-depressants.

Richard's wife, Lee, said: 'We had our house vandalised – paint bombs and everything. Our close neighbours believed us and knew it wasn't Richard and we reported the incidents to police but nothing was done. We didn't know who it was.'

Richard also had to face the stares of people near their home and after two months, the couple were forced to pack their bags and leave the town. 'We moved to Fort William six years ago and had built a life but we had to leave. We had just had enough,' said Richard. 'I knew I had no reason to hide but I felt I always needed to watch my back. I ended up ill and in hospital over it.'

Why his twin decided to implicate Richard remained a mystery to the innocent man: 'I don't know what was on my brother's mind. I went to see him in prison when he was on remand. It hurt me seeing him there. He never mentioned his defence to me and hasn't explained why he said it. His wife is standing by him and I will stand by him. He has committed a serious crime and he has to pay for it and do his time. I know what he has done and my heart goes out to his victim… I can't even look in the mirror now. All I see is my brother.'

Remarkably, Richard was still able to talk with affection about his devious twin. 'I couldn't believe it when I was told my brother was planning to use me to try to get away with this. It was very upsetting and very hurtful. But, despite that, I love him to bits. He is my brother. I know what he has done but I will stand by him no matter what.'

Even as Richard Greens was pondering his twin's actions, Robert was cockily taking bets inside Edinburgh's Saughton Prison that he would not receive a life sentence. The sentence on Greens had been deferred for background reports – including an investigation into the risks that he might strike again – and he was running a book with fellow cons. One prison source said: 'He's offering tobacco and phone cards to anyone willing to take the bet. If he doesn't get life, they have to pay. Greens is even saying he'll get no more than a two-year stretch. But we reckon he's in for a big surprise when he goes back in front of the judge.'

And he was – he got ten years. Judge Lord Mackay told the High Court that he had considered 'very fully and very anxiously' whether Greens should get a life sentence for the 'brutal and violent' attack. In his court defence QC Donald Findlay had said Greens had experienced 'feelings of self-disgust' and had become distressed when talking about the attack. In the end Lord Mackay made an order that Greens should be kept under strict supervision for seven years after the end of his prison term. He said: 'The sentence I am about to impose is intended not only to punish you for what you did. It will also mark society's condemnation for what you did.'

Fortunately the DNA evidence did not have to be debated in court, but three officers who worked on the investigation were later commended by the Lothian and Borders Chief Constable. Inspector Millar, Sergeant Andrew Waddell and Constable Gaynor Bain 'worked tirelessly to investigate and prepare evidence' the force said.

7

THE FAT RIPPER

S ome murderers stand in the dock hoping that the tiny scrap of evidence that links them to their crime might be disputed or discredited and that they will then walk free. Perhaps that is why Philip Smith, 6ft 4in tall and weighing 22 stone, decided to plead not guilty to the horrific and brutal murder of three women in four days – crimes that earned him the name 'The Fat Ripper'.

If so, he was mistaken. Because the evidence against Smith was so overwhelming that even the most experienced forensic officers involved in the case felt their only problem was that they almost had too much evidence to prove him guilty. Their main difficulty was sifting through it all!

Philip John Smith was born on 10 July 1965 at the City Maternity Hospital in Gloucester. His father, sawmill labourer Henry Smith, and mother, Rose Luckins, both gave their addresses as caravan sites. The eldest of the couple's five surviving children, he grew up in the city's deprived Coney Hill Estate. The plight of the Smith family worsened when Henry was in a road accident on the way to a funfair where he was then working. He was so badly hurt that he fell into a coma for six weeks. Afterwards he was left unable to talk, having bitten his tongue off in the crash.

Poorly educated, Smith attended a special school and left at 14 without any qualifications, but even then he had been showing strange tendencies for years. At the age of eight, he took delight in setting fire to a string of sympathy cards for his three-year-old sister who had died from leukaemia. They had been attached to the chimney breast and his frightened mother had to put the fire out. As he grew up he would set fire to wood, fences or a shed in the back garden and watch the fire brigade come to fight the blaze. He also showed a violent side. He once lashed out at his brother Paul and broke his leg, even putting his sister Janet in hospital with broken ribs after they'd had a row.

In 1989, by now 24, Smith met Shelagh Tingle while running a darts stall at a travelling fair that visited her home town of Ross-on-Wye, Herefordshire. The couple then lived together in the nearby village of Walford or travelled across the country with Billy Danter's Fun Fair. They had three children: in 1990 a boy, and two years later, twin girls. All three were quickly taken into care and subsequently adopted, and the couple split up after just a few years together.

Working as an itinerant fairground worker, Smith then

spent time in Athlone, Ireland, staying with travellers he met there, sleeping in a spare caravan and paying £20 a week towards his food. Sometimes, if still hungry after a meal, he would wolf down a tin of cold Ambrosia rice pudding. He said he was an English gypsy who enjoyed wandering across Ireland, but his tendencies were already beginning to emerge in the remarks he made to the young girls he encountered. If they changed their clothes he would tell them he preferred the ones with more cleavage showing – the kind of thing you just didn't say to girls from communities such as the travellers.

Eventually, in 1999, he arrived in Birmingham, staying initially in a hostel for the homeless and then in a three-storey housing association home in Braithwaite Road, half a mile from the city centre. The most terrible chapter in his violent life was about to begin.

Smith, who still had his soft Gloucestershire burr, drank in the numerous pubs of the less reputable parts of the city. He regularly visited the Rainbow pub in Digbeth near the city centre, where he would sometimes drive customers home for payment and carry out odd jobs for the landlady. Meal times would find him eating alone at the Shamrock Cafe on Stratford Road, just around the corner from his flat. Café-owner Jim Smith was to recall: 'He was a gentle giant who we named "Bigfoot" because his boots always used to leave black marks on the floor. Ninety-nine per cent of the time he had a dirty appearance and looked like he had been working on a car.'

But the lumbering Smith was no gentle giant. In fact he

was a bully and a man with an enormous and uncontrollable temper that was about to erupt.

It was just after 6.15am on 9 November 2000 when PC Kevin Rumley and another officer on mobile patrol saw smoke at some parkland near the Ackers Trust Ski Centre in Sparkbrook, a fairly run-down district not far from the city centre. They went to investigate on foot and PC Rumley was later to say: 'I shone my torch in the direction of the smoke coming from behind the railings and saw a human body which was smouldering. My first impression was that it was the body of a woman. The legs were drawn up to the knees, flames were still flickering near the abdomen.'

After the Fire Brigade had doused the flames, a horrifying sight greeted them all. It was the charred body of 21-year-old drug addict Jodie Hyde, who had been stripped, wrapped in a blanket tied with rope, covered in petrol and set alight, burning 60 per cent of her body. She had been strangled to death, almost certainly by hand, and there were marks on her pitiful body consistent with her putting up a struggle. Hyde, who had once appeared in a BBC documentary about butane gas abuse, had lived alone in a flat with her dog Toby, and Smith had probably killed her at his flat before deciding to dump her body.

Smith was a habitué of the sleazy parts of Birmingham and the second murder in his 72 hours of mayhem started with a row outside the Monte Carlo Club on the notorious Soho Road in Handsworth. In the early hours of 12 November, Smith had an argument with Rosemary Corcoran that was captured on CCTV. Like poor Jodie Hyde, Corcoran, who had been drinking heavily, was a woman Smith knew from his pub haunts. Indeed he had been with them both at The Rainbow on the nights before they died.

PCs Jonathan Richards and Martin Maynard came across Smith and Corcoran at 4.40am. PC Richards later said: 'This man was holding the female back. She looked like she was trying to go back to the club and he was manhandling her away. I was en route to another job but I spoke to Miss Corcoran and asked if everything was OK. There were physically no signs of injury but she did appear agitated and distressed, as well as drunk.

'At first the man did not acknowledge we were there, but then he turned and said there was no problem. I asked her if she had been hurt and she said no. Neither wanted to talk to us so we left for the other job. As he left, the man kept saying over and over: "Do you think I would let someone hurt my missus?"'

Four hours later the 5ft 3in brunette's body was found by a man walking his dog in a lane near the Rashwood Nursing Home in Droitwich, about 30 minutes drive from the club on the quiet, early Sunday roads. The site was near Junction 5 of the M5 motorway to Birmingham, so it was easily and quickly reached from the city centre.

Corcoran, a 25-year-old mother of three, had died as a result of massive head and neck injuries. Her face had literally been shattered and she was stripped of anything that might identify her. Only fingerprints, and dental records after her jaw was reassembled, enabled police to establish her identity. Smith had driven to a garage and filed a can with petrol with the intention of setting her body alight, but changed his mind. It proved to be a fatal decision for his third victim, 39-year-old Carol Jordan, because it meant that a few hours later she and Smith were in the same place at the same time.

Care-worker Carol, a married mother of six, was on her way to a home for the elderly for her 8 am to 1 pm shift. She liked to work those hours as she felt safer walking to the home in daylight. She was only 100 yards from her home when Smith drove his Volvo estate into her on Bell Barn Road, causing her serious head and leg injuries. The giant Smith then carried his 5ft 1in, eight-stone victim 150 yards to a secluded grassed area, where he battered her to death, probably with a brick, causing 38 injuries in total and 15 to her head alone. It was at about the time his second victim's body was being discovered, and his second slaying within a few hours on that Remembrance Sunday morning. Unlike his other two victims, Carol, described as 'a dedicated wife and mother', did not even know the man who killed her.

Astonishingly Smith contacted police within a day of the discovery of Rosemary Corcoran's battered body, after staff at the Rainbow told him that she was missing. For some bizarre reason, perhaps fearing he would be linked with her anyway and anxious to appear innocent, on 13 November he decided to telephone the police at Castle Vale in Birmingham to give a statement about her disappearance – before her body had even been identified.

The untruths he told were to help trap him. Detective Constable Ruth Wilkins later recalled how Smith had phoned at 4pm. She said: 'He said he would like to come to the police station to help with the inquiry and that he had seen her on Saturday night leave the pub with an unknown man. He insisted he would like to come over to the police station. He said he had been asked to contact the police by someone else and gave his mobile number.'

Within the hour Smith had arrived at the station and given a short statement trying to cover his tracks and his crimes with a mixture of lies and half-truths. It was one of the few occasions he was to even speak to the police about the events of those 72 hours. Later he was to stay silent about what exactly happened.

He said he'd gone to the Rainbow pub with Miss Corcoran and a male friend of hers before they had all moved on to the Kerryman pub in Digbeth. This much was true, and Smith also told the truth when he described how Corcoran's friend was thrown out of the Kerryman.

But then he told police: 'At about 1.50am we left the Kerryman and went to a nightclub called Monte's. I parked my car and we walked across to the nightclub. We were seated next to the bar and Rosie had a vodka and orange. After 30 minutes Rosie asked me to go up and dance. Rosie then started dancing with two black males. I was sitting at a table just off the dance floor. She was dancing with them for around 30 minutes. It was very dark. They were dancing in a 'dirty dancing' style, rubbing their bodies against each other. Rosie came back over to me still leaving the males dancing. She asked if I would go and get the coats, which I did. We went outside the nightclub into the street.'

It was then, he said, that a teddy boy – who Rosie had argued with at the Kerryman pub over her friend's ejection – turned up and became aggressive. 'Rosie was leaning against the wall and was still drunk. She slipped on the floor and a police car approached. I said to Rosie: "Are you coming home?" Rosie replied: "I am not going home." I felt that I could not persuade her to go so I decided to leave without her. I felt uneasy but had to get up the next morning. The black males had been standing nearby. She stood up and I drove off down the hill from Rosie. I believe she wanted to go with them.'

These were lies, and he ended with the biggest lie of all, saying: 'I have made this statement in the hope that it will help the police find Rosie safe and well.' It was just 24 hours since had killed her.

Even then, however, the evidence was mounting against him. Smith had been seen leaving the Rainbow pub with both Jodie Hyde and then Rosemary Corcoran on the days before they were found dead. In fact, he was the last person known to have seen either of them alive and that immediately made him a suspect.

CCTV footage from across the city picked up Smith's blue car in key locations on the day of Jodie Hyde's murder. It showed her getting out to visit a chemist and later being driven about by Smith, who was also pictured buying petrol in a filling can from a garage. The car was later shown driving to and from the murder scene where he set Miss Hyde's body alight.

Then there was the footage that showed him struggling

with Rosie Corcoran outside the nightclub in Handsworth and driving around Bromsgrove after killing her in Droitwich. One motorist recalled seeing Smith, with blood on him, buying petrol in a can. Another noticed Smith had no marks on his hands despite insisting he had been in a fight. Cameras then captured him on his way back to Birmingham, which was where he ran over Carol Jordan and then brutally beat her to death.

More than a dozen bloodstains from the victims were found on his car, clothing and in his flat. Even the boots he used to savagely kick Rosie Corcoran and Carol Jordan still had their blood splattered on them when he was arrested. A bag of Jodie Hyde's items was found outside his flat. To make matters worse for him he had tried to clean his clothes in the bath, along with a pair of Rosie Corcoran's trousers. When officers arrived at his flat they found them still soaking – and still bloodstained.

His Volvo estate had four different types of tyres on it and they matched the Droitwich murder scene tyre marks – and the traces on Rosie Corcoran's body itself where he had run over her. Fragments from a light-cluster that had been damaged when he hit Mrs Jordan were found and matched exactly the broken unit, which Smith had simply put in the boot of his car. Paint specks on her jacket were the same as those from the Volvo. And there was more – more than 100 exhibits of evidence had been gathered by police, who had also viewed hundreds of hours of CCTV footage.

The already strong case was bolstered by scores of blood and DNA samples, analysed and linked to Smith by scientists at the Forensic Science Service (FSS) in Birmingham. It seemed a watertight case against an evil man who had left a trail of incriminating clues, but when he appeared at Leicester Crown Court on 3 July 2001, Smith – who had refused to talk to detectives after his arrest – pleaded not guilty to the three murders, claiming that the police had tampered with vital forensic evidence and that a mystery man may have been using his car.

As the jury heard mounting evidence of his guilt, Smith, scruffy and often unshaven in a blue T-shirt and jeans, looked straight ahead and avoided the gaze of the families of his victims as they sat in court. There had been an application before the trial began that he should be handcuffed throughout the hearing, but the judge ruled against it on the grounds it might prejudice the jury. So, for security reasons, he was guarded in the dock by four prison officers.

When questioned by his defence counsel, he spoke softly with his Gloucestershire accent barely audible at times, but when cross-examined by the prosecution he started to become agitated and avoided answering concisely. After just a few minutes of interrogation he said he felt unwell and complained of a pain in his eyes and chest pains. When he returned after being treated by a doctor, he was sluggish and slurred his words. Smith then complained his eyes were hurting, and asked to speak to his barrister. The judge refused his request.

The trial then took an astonishing turn when the 22-stone monster stunned the court by saying: 'I need to change my plea. I'm fed up with this. I want to change my plea.' When

Smith's guilty plea was subsequently submitted, there were gasps and crying in the public gallery. Even as relatives of his victims sobbed and stifled cheers, Smith remained impassive in the dock.

He also stood unmoved with arms folded as he was sentenced by the judge, Mrs Justice Rafferty. 'Philip John Smith,' she said, 'you robbed three innocent ladies of their lives. I suspect that the families will suffer all the more because they simply do not understand why you did what you did. The brutality of these ladies' deaths was designed by you to evade discovery. The coldness by which you despatched them is appalling. You should have faced up like a man to the overwhelming nature of the Crown's evidence much earlier. But you chose to put the families through misery, which you compounded by this trial. There is no sentence other than that I now impose on you on all three counts and that is that you will go to prison for life. Take him down.'

At the end of the trial Jim Taylor, elder brother of Carol Jordan said: 'I would like to just ask Smith one question – why Carol? We are all hoping that Philip Smith will never – and I mean never – be allowed into the outside world ever again.'

Meanwhile West Midlands Chief Constable Sir Edward Crew paid tribute to the work of his detectives and said, as is often the case in crimes where DNA has been a factor: 'Our operation continues because Smith is a wicked man who callously took the lives of three women and there is good reason to believe he may be responsible for serious crimes against a number of others. We are seeking to uncover the full extent of his criminality by working closely with other police forces as well as the Forensic Science Service and the National Crime Faculty.'

By any standards, the evidence against Smith had been massive, prompting senior forensic scientist Martin Whittaker, who coordinated the case for the FSS, to say: 'A team of forensic scientists from different specialities worked really hard to gather everything they could. The team pulled together every strand of forensic evidence to create a kind of spider's web and in the centre of it all, linked to each one of the murdered women, was Philip Smith. This was a difficult case to deal with because there was so much evidence to look at. In 20 years of working for the FSS, I have never had to deal with so much in relation to one suspect – it was quite overwhelming. But the results of our work gave police a very strong case against Smith. Throughout the investigation, the FSS and the police worked very closely together and the result is a tribute to that partnership.'

The FSS had been called in to assist West Midlands Police with their expert scientific support after the discovery of the burnt body of Jodie Hyde. Two members of staff, one a senior forensic scene examiner and the other a DNA expert, had gone to the scene and the post mortem to advise, among other things, on the taking of samples. Three days later the on-call forensic scene examiner was called to Droitwich by West Mercia Police when the body of Rosie Corcoran was found in a secluded lane. The scientist was carrying out an examination of the blood distribution at the scene when he received a call to attend the scene of another murder – that of Mrs Jordan in Birmingham.

Initially the three murders were treated by police as entirely separate, as there was nothing about them to suggest a link. Once Smith was arrested, however, two FSS scientists visited his home in Braithwaite Road, and another examined his Volvo car and searched for evidence. The evidence recovered was crucial to the case and linked him to all three women's deaths. At Smith's home, they found the bath full of murky, brown water that contained bloodstained clothing. Back at the FSS lab in Birmingham, scientists examined items from his home and the crime scenes and found many links between the suspect and the three murders.

But there is one more fascinating fact about the seedy, violent life of Philip Smith; his coincidental link to one of the most notorious serial killers in British criminal history, Fred West. The association began when Smith's then-unmarried mother Maggie worked as a cleaner in a hotel at the same time as handyman John West – brother of the House of Horrors killer – was employed there. Maggie lived in the quiet Herefordshire town of Ledbury. John West, like his older brother Fred, was born in the village of Much Marcle, five miles away, and as they grew up the West brothers would spend their nights out in Ledbury.

The paths of the families were to cross after Maggie's marriage and the Smiths moved to a flat at No.21 Midland Road, Gloucester. (It was during this time, in 1965, that Smith was born.) In April 1970, Fred West and his future wife Rosemary Letts moved in just up the road when they rented a one-bedroom flat at No.10. Three months later, they moved even closer when they got to a bigger flat at No.25. In 1971, the Smith family moved and a year later the Wests went to 25 Cromwell Street – the House of Horrors.

Then, in 1990 Smith, now aged 25, moved into a bed-sit in Cromwell Street. His sister Janet was to say: 'I know Philip knew Fred West – because he told me so. But he didn't mention his name when he was living in Cromwell Street. It just came out when Fred West was arrested.'

It is one bizarre footnote in the vicious lives of both men that they should have lived so near each other in the same nondescript street in a quiet English town – and then gone on to terrify and murder a string of helpless victims.

8

THE SEX-MAD DJ

One thing most people seemed to agree on was that DJ Richard Baker had no trouble pulling the girls. He was good-looking, affable, at ease with women and certainly in possession of the gift of the gab.

His lifestyle was perfect too. For long periods he worked in Torremolinos where the living – and the laying – was easy. Besotted girl tourists, holiday trade workers and many more besides fell under his spell as he spent his days on the beach toning his athletic body and his nights in the Spanish discotheques. But beneath that exterior sophistication and liking for the ladies was a monster who craved sex – and didn't care how he got it.

Baker's story is one of the most remarkable in the ever-increasing use of genetics to trap wrongdoers. For not only did DNA help nail him, it was his own brother who acted to put him behind bars.

Baker grew up in Camelford, on the edge of Bodmin Moor in Cornwall, an area once renowned for its smuggling and made famous by Daphne du Maurier's novel, *Jamaica Inn*. His parents divorced when he was eight, and he and his older brother Kevin went to live with their mother, who was later to marry a wealthy estate agent, in Bodmin. Baker left school with seven O-levels and trained as an electrician before deciding to set up his own DJ business. Even in those days he was known as a hunky 'Jack the Lad' by the local girls. One was later to recall: 'Everyone was into Wham! then and Richard looked just like George Michael. He knew he was good-looking and any girl that went to him with a request would be chatted up. When girls walked into pubs he always shouted out, "Hey babes!"'

An early girlfriend of Baker's said: 'He was very good-looking and charming, but a prat as well. He always had lots of girls on the side.'

The local girls were getting to know him, but so were the local police. By 1983 he had twice been fined for theft and the following year he was given community service for assault and causing bodily harm.

A foretaste of the perversions that lay ahead came in December 1986 when he raped a 19-year-old girl in Bideford, Devon. He and his brother Kevin were working with a travelling fair when he pounced on her as she walked home late at night. Baker was later given six years by Exeter Crown Court, while Kevin, who sat in a van nearby while the attack happened, got four years for aiding and abetting.

While he was in jail Baker was visited by a local girl, Kathy

Walsh. He persuaded her he was innocent and when he was released in 1991 the pair set up home together, living at first with Baker's mother but later moving to Plymouth. By day he worked as an insurance salesman and by night as a DJ in the city's clubs.

He got engaged to Kathy and the pair planned to marry in May 1992, but two days before the wedding Baker was arrested and accused of raping a prostitute in Bristol. Although he was acquitted after she continually failed to turn up at court, Kathy eventually broke up with him in 1994 after he was charged with raping another vice girl he had picked up after a stint as a DJ in a Plymouth wine bar. She said he had refused to pay her and then forced her to have sex. Baker tried to make her drop her complaint by offering her a £6,500 bribe. He was later cleared of rape but was jailed for four years for trying to pervert the course of justice. He also confessed to having unlawful sex with a 15-year-old girl who was on work experience with his insurance company. After the case, the prostitute yelled at Baker's mother: 'What kind of a monster have you bred?'

Baker was freed from jail in July 1997 and decided to reinvent himself. And what better place to do so than sunny Spain? Torremolinos was the perfect place for Baker to seek work. As an entertainer he could get close to hundreds of girls who flock to the Costa del Sol resort every year.

British police had been alerted by someone who saw Baker applying for a job in the town and they immediately warned their colleagues abroad. Within a few weeks of his arrival, the local police were on the look-out for him.

Baker's first job was handing out leaflets for the dozens of bars and clubs in the area. He was in his thirties by now while many of the people he worked with were still in their teens or early twenties, but he would explain the age gap by saying he was trying to recover from a broken engagement. His good looks, easy manner and ability to speak both German and Spanish made him a hit with teenage girls from all over Europe. Antonio Martinez, manager of the Beach Club Hotel where Baker worked, later said: 'He was always surrounded by girls, he loved it. He would trot out this line about the girl being "very lovely". It wasn't clever but it would work.'

Spanish police had been trying without success to trace him since his arrival in the country, but in November 1997 he did their work for them by asking the local police for a work and residence permit.

Jose Cabrera, the police commissioner, for the area said: 'Unfortunately Torremolinos is the perfect hunting ground for a rapist. The combination of holiday atmosphere, number of tourists, easy access to drink and drugs, and casual attitudes towards sex makes the job of catching a rapist and making the charge stick a difficult one. Every summer we have a number of reported rapes, but in most cases the victim and the attacker turn out to be too drunk to remember what happened, and the charges are dropped. Richard Baker was different. We had a sex maniac on the loose. He is cold, calculating, intelligent and obsessed with sex.'

When he was told of Baker's eventual arrest in England, Senor Cabrera said: 'In my 30 years as a police officer, I have never been so worried about the actions of one individual as

I was about Richard Baker. He was a time bomb. I was convinced that one day he would have killed.'

Juan Fernandez, who was employed in the bar next to the Fun Club where Baker also worked, said: 'He told girls if they said anything he'd kill them. Richard took a lot of drugs, especially cocaine. He had a real problem with coke and sex. He needed both all the time.'

Keyboard player Norman Green, who also worked with Baker, said: 'He was always boasting about his sex exploits with girls he took to the beach. They were aged about 16 to 13, maybe not even that. Sometimes he'd take three, come back and say: "They wanted it so I gave it to them." They were never over the age of consent.'

A barman who saw Baker's photographs said: 'There were at least 10 different girls and they all looked drugged and out of it. Some were naked. It was foul.'

Once the police knew where he was, he was put under surveillance, but it came to nothing as he continually journeyed between Spain and Britain. Then in June 1998, two Swedish girls went to police in Marbella and reported that they had been raped in Torremolinos. The two friends had been on a two-week holiday when they met a young man called Ricardo who invited them to a night out in the town, where he was working as a DJ. The next thing they remember clearly is waking up in the morning next to each other in a bed in a strange flat. They were both naked and realised they had both been sexually assaulted.

When the case landed on the desk of Chief Inspector Juan Antonio Blanco, he already had a feeling who Ricardo might be. When one of the girls produced a picture of her with Ricardo's arms around her waist, he knew Baker had struck again. The police suspected he had used the date-drug Rohypnol, which makes the victim drowsy, leaving them with a blurred memory of recent events. Baker was eventually arrested but was released without charge after claiming that the two girls consented to sex. Under interrogation, the police said, he gave a 'chilling performance'.

One recalled: 'Both his solicitor and interpreter were women. Baker began to brag to them about his sexual prowess. Then he graphically told of every sex act he performed on the girl. As he spoke, he smirked at the women. He was getting a thrill making them squirm.' Lacking sufficient evidence to charge him, the police freed Baker, who next began making trips back to Britain to seek out 'hostesses' to whom he would offer work on the Costa.

It was back in England that Baker's reign of terror was to begin – and where he was eventually to be captured in the most remarkable circumstances. In seven terrifying months he carried out a series of at least 12 attacks on women in various parts of the country. But the DNA collected from several of these incidents told detectives that the attacks were being carried out by the same man. It was this information that enabled them to focus their enquiries.

The timetable of terror that an Old Bailey jury was eventually to hear makes chilling reading. It read like this, with his victims' names not being revealed as is customary in cases of sexual assault and rape:

MISS A, 22, was attacked in Kilburn, Northwest London,

on 13 May 1998 after she got off a tube train at nearby Willesden Green and began walking home. The attack happened just 10 days after she had moved to London from Yorkshire. The young victim said Baker had grabbed her by the neck. 'He kept repeating that he wasn't going to hurt me, he wasn't going to rape me.' As she screamed, she was told: 'Shut up, or I will kill you.' He indecently assaulted her then began crying, telling her: 'I have never done this before. I feel really stupid.'

MISS B, 35, was attacked six days later as she left Highgate tube station in North London. Baker put his hand around her neck and told her: 'I just want to hold you. If you struggle, I will kill you.' But she managed to wriggle free.

MISS C, 16, became his first rape victim on 23 May. She was walking to meet her mother at a community centre in Kentish Town, North London, when Baker ran up behind her. 'He grabbed me around my neck and he held my mouth. He was behind me and he started unbuttoning my top. He said that if I was going to shout he would kill me.' She was ordered to give her name, age and address and then Baker lifted her T-shirt over her head so she could not see him.

She said: 'I asked him not to rape me and he said he was not going to rape me and that he was just a dirty old man.' But he did rape the girl and told her: 'Don't tell anyone about this or I will kill you. If I see it in the newspapers or on the news, I will come looking for you.' He said he had seen her in school uniform and knew where she lived and her route home.

MISS D, 18, was raped outside her home in Brighton,

Sussex, after she had locked herself out. Baker allegedly told her: 'If you run away I will catch you. You have high heels on and you will never make it and I will kill you,' adding 'This isn't rape. Rape is beating you black and blue and leaving you for dead.' Afterwards, the girl cowered behind a van all night before her flatmate returned home and found her. Later, she picked out Baker at an identity parade.

MISS E, 15, was raped two days later in Southend, Essex, as she walked home after partying with friends. Her attacker told her: 'I can run faster than you in your high heels.' After raping her, Baker forced her to say that she had enjoyed the attack.

MISS F, 16, was attacked in Southend on 11 September after a row with her boyfriend. Fortunately he turned up and fought Baker off.

MISS G, 21, was attacked just one hour later. Baker fondled her before telling a bogus sob story about his wife walking out on him with their two children.

MISS H, 26, was raped at about 4.30am the following day after leaving a casino in North London where she worked. Baker pulled her into a garden where he forced her to have sex. He then told her lies about his wife having an affair with his best man.

MISS I, 21, was attacked near a tube station in East London on 28 October. Again her attacker made a remark about her not being able to run away in high heels. He fled when she screamed as he indecently assaulted her.

MISS J, 22, was attacked in her home in North London. After she was indecently assaulted she heard a noise downstairs and her attacker fled.

MISS K, 25, was attacked in the hallway of a block of flats in North London and was told: 'Don't scream or I will kill you.' After the assault, Baker told her: 'My wife was killed. I lost my best friend and I lost my job.'

MISS L, the final victim, was attacked in Regent's Park, North London, but managed to fight Baker off.

The DNA collected from saliva and semen proved that it was one man carrying out these attacks, but detectives still had to catch him. That capture came about in the most remarkable way.

Essex Police were the first to spot a pattern to the sex attacks that had taken place in Southend-on-Sea, including the rape of the 15-year-old in a car park. The method of assault was almost always the same: Baker attacked his victim from behind, put an arm around her neck and threatened to kill her if she screamed or tried to run away. Setting up Operation Monarch, they contacted other forces to find further cases. The Metropolitan Police and the Sussex Police soon joined the operation after similar attacks in Brighton and London. The DNA evidence from his victims enabled detectives throughout the areas to be certain that one man had raped or assaulted 12 women over an eight-month period in 1998. Whoever was carrying out the attacks seemed to be out of control and had to be caught – and quickly.

The breakthrough came in dramatic fashion as Jill Dando and her team prepared to highlight the case on BBC's *Crimewatch*. Before it was transmitted, however, Baker was shopped to police by his brother Kevin, 36, who had seen trailers for the programme and recognised an e-fit picture of the attacker. Now a successful West Country businessman, Kevin Baker rang the incident room to give detectives his brother's name and tell them he was staying with their mother in Bodmin.

One source close to the case said: 'He had been in trouble with Richard many years ago but had put it all in the past and wanted to put an end to his brother's activities. When he saw the *Crimewatch* programme he was appalled by what his brother had been doing.'

Officers from London rang colleagues in the Devon and Cornwall but they found Baker had already left on a coach for Heathrow Airport. His description was sent to London and as the coach pulled up in the early hours of 16 December, detectives were waiting. Among them was Detective Sergeant Peter Bartlett – one of the officers who had helped prepare the Crimewatch item. 'I spotted him coming off the coach. He had high cheekbones and dark looks. I was sure we had our man.'

The senior investigating officer, Detective Superintendent David Bright of Essex Police, said: 'It was a fantastic breakthrough, just what we had been waiting for. Jill Dando and her team did a marvellous job. Millions of people saw it and we received valuable information in addition to the name of the attacker.'

After his arrest Baker refused to answer questions, merely telling detectives: 'It was not me.'

British police officers subsequently travelled to Spain where they discovered that Baker had been arrested twice after three young women had complained to Torremolinos police that he had raped them after sedating them, almost certainly with the 'date rape' drug Rohypnol.

In addition to the two Swedish girls, there had been a second incident a month later, when a 17-year-old Swedish girl reported that she had been raped the night before by an Englishman who called himself Richard. She too remembered little of what had happened and was taken to hospital for tests. But she was afraid to press charges, and did not contest Baker's claim that she had consented to having sex with him. After a night in the cells, Baker went before the judge, and once again was freed. Police later found Rohypnol among Baker's possessions.

At his trial in England, Baker admitted a string of indecent assaults on victims who were forced to strip before being fondled and made to perform oral sex. But he denied four rapes, two indecent assaults and one attempted indecent assault. That meant that his victims had to relive their ordeals in court. Their tales were all harrowing, but Baker's evidence offers a glimpse inside his warped mind.

He described how he targeted his young victims, waiting until it got dark: 'I wouldn't plan it for weeks on end. It was usually spontaneous, a spur of the moment thing. I wouldn't say: "It's 4.30, I must attack a woman."

'I tried to terrorise my victims. I tried to put so much fear into them. I wanted to be totally in control and make sure they wouldn't resist me or put up a fight or a struggle so I could terrorise them. I terrorised these poor girls, I know I did. I would threaten them that if they went to the police there would be trouble. "If you go to the police I will kill you." I tried to put so much fear in them. I just wanted to see their reaction.'

He admitted telling one young woman during her ordeal: 'This isn't rape. Rape is battering you black and blue and leaving you for dead.'

He admitted to his own counsel, Oliver Blunt, QC, that he had attacked the four women who claimed to have been raped, but said it had stopped short of full sex. One woman was made to 'get on all fours and wiggle'. Baker said: 'I like that position. For me it's the position I like to look at a girl, on all fours. I asked her to put her g-string back and I was a bit of a voyeur, I suppose.'

During his evidence, Baker was asked whether he enjoyed acts described by his own counsel as 'depraved'.

He replied in a whisper: 'Very much'.

Cross-examined by prosecutor Nicholas Hilliard, Baker said he often paid the women compliments. He looked up at one alleged victim, casino croupier Miss H, 26, and said: 'I think I paid her a compliment, yes. I don't know why. I probably found them attractive, their figure, their hair, their looks.' Staring directly at Miss H, he said: 'I did tell her in particular.'

Mr Hilliard: 'In your life you have had a number of girlfriends, haven't you?'

Baker: 'Yes, sir.'

Mr Hilliard: 'It's fair to say, a large number of girlfriends?'

Baker: 'Yes, sir.'

Mr Hilliard: 'You had sex with them?'

Baker: 'Yes, sir.'

But he admitted that he still went out looking for women to attack and would grab them around the neck before forcing them to commit indecent acts. Asked why, he replied: 'I just wanted to be in control.'

Mr Hilliard asked whether Baker regretted his crimes and he replied: 'At that time, no, sir.'

'When?' asked Mr Hilliard.

Baker replied: 'When I was arrested and imprisoned, the realisation of what I had done. I still think about what I had done.'

Asked to detail his planning, he said that on one occasion he was eating fish and chips in Southend before attacking one woman. 'I was thinking lots of things. I'm eating fish and chips. I went to play a couple of slot machines. Then later in the evening as it has got darker I have thoughts about something.'

Mr Hilliard asked: 'How do you select a victim?'

Baker said: 'Generally, you know… just a lone female. As you know, the ages here range from 15 to 35. A young person, around 20, I would generally seek. I have followed them for a short distance and some longer, yes, sir.'

Detailing the attacks he admitted to saying: 'I would either say: 'Don't scream' or 'Be quiet.' I would follow it up with a threat.'

When Mr Hilliard pointed out that this method was also used in the attacks he denied, Baker replied: 'Maybe he did the same. How many ways can somebody grab a woman?'

The prosecutor accused him of lying to avoid responsibility for his crimes.

'No, sir,' he replied. But he admitted lying to his victims to try and cover his tracks. He made up bogus sob stories about members of his family dying. 'It was all lies. I lied to all the girls.'

He added: 'I always told them I wouldn't rape them. I told them I wouldn't and I haven't. I liked to touch them either on the breasts or on the vagina. I would lie to the girls I have grabbed and I would make up a story. I would pretend I was local or from nearby or I would lie and say I was at university or say about my family – personal things deliberately giving them the wrong information.'

Mr Hilliard the accused him of telling a pack of lies to his victims.

Baker replied: 'Yes, absolutely.'

Mr Hilliard: 'Will you accept that you are a thoroughly dishonest person?' Baker: 'I'm dishonest in that I lied to all the girls.'

Mr Hilliard: 'You are a thief and a robber?'

Baker: 'Yes, I am.'

Despite his denials it came as no surprise that Baker was found guilty in May 1999 and the following month was given four life sentences for his crimes by the judge, Recorder David Stokes. He received a total of 49 years for the other attacks to run alongside the life sentences. He was told he must serve 12 years and 5 months before even being considered for parole.

He was a 'practised and plausible liar' the judge told him, adding: 'Your conduct was appalling.' He said Baker had written to him from prison admitting he had lied during the case and that the victims had told the truth. But he believed Baker either could not care less what happened to his victims or had been unable to understand the effects his actions had on them. 'You treated women with complete contempt. You are not mentally ill but you are in my opinion a truly depraved and wicked man who is a danger to women for the foreseeable future. I consider the circumstances of these attacks and indecent assaults are exceptional as to the number, the period over which they were carried out and the sheer nastiness of them. I have the public to think about.'

Baker burst into tears as he was sentenced and his brother Kevin shouted from the public gallery: 'Justice has been done!' Many of the DJ's victims were in the same room to see him jailed and the 26-year-old who suffered a 90-minute rape ordeal said she was not fooled by Baker's tears. 'I take them with a pinch of salt,' she said. 'I'm not sure they were real. He can be very plausible. Twelve years is not a lot compared to life. I'm sorry it wasn't longer.'

The 16-year-old raped by Baker in north London said: 'I don't want him ever to be back on the streets. It wouldn't be safe for women. He has wrecked my life – I have lost all my confidence.'

After Baker's conviction, his brother revealed in an interview what had made him snitch on his brother. 'Most of the time he seduced girls and had sex with them on the beach or in the nightclub toilets. Most of them were vastly under-age – he didn't care. Richard always told people he was 26 and he's really 34. He targeted young girls who were with their family. They loved him because he is good-looking and a DJ and living in a holiday resort.

'He was really sneaky. He would spot a couple of young girls, maybe 13 or 14, and then befriend their family. The parents then entrusted him to look after the girls at the nightclub and of course he would abuse that trust and give them Rohypnol and have sex with them. There was one time I remember Richard not only seduced the daughter but had sex with the mum as well.

'He even showed me photos he had taken. Some were of very young girls, aged about 13, naked in his bed. Some of them showed three girls lying together who were obviously under the influence of drugs. Because of the Rohypnol he regularly had two or three girls at a time and he bragged about it. He would tell me that he had this one or that, and her sister and her mother. It was never-ending. He also bragged how he had bedded a string of Brazilian dancers who performed a show at the hotel complex once a week and he had also slept with six Swedish girls.

'I was letting him think I approved where really I was plotting to get him caught. I thought he is not going to get away with this. I called a friend at home who is a female police officer and she told me to get proof. When I got back after the week's holiday I contacted Devon and Cornwall Police but they said there was nothing they could do about it because I had no evidence. I spoke to the police about the Rohypnol and they told me to prove it. I started to work with the woman officer to get him caught because he used to come back into the country with drugs. They tried to arrest him for importing drugs but whenever they searched he never had anything on him.

'I then contacted *Crimewatch* because a couple of rapes that had been reported sounded just like Richard of old. I also started putting together some dates and times of rapes and comparing them with whether Richard was in or out of the country at the time. I spoke to the police again because I knew that he was involved somehow in a number of rapes where they have never been solved. But I think the problem was that Richard had been clever enough to spread the rapes all over the country.

'Richard arrived at mum's place in Bodmin on 12 December. When I saw him he had scars on his hands and I asked if he had got the injuries running away from someone. He confessed he had forced sex with a girl on a National Express coach from London down to the south coast. The following day I called the police and they then arrested him on 16 December. I knew it was Richard so I rang *Crimewatch*.

'I then rang Richard and tried to keep him in the area but he told me that he was leaving for Spain and he gave me the time and place of the flight. I told the police if they didn't catch him then they would never catch him. He was going to Spain and then on to South Africa. I keep a very detailed diary and without me and my cooperation they would never have caught Richard.'

Baker's mother, Lesley Hamley, admitted that after an earlier conviction for a sex offence Richard had told her he realised he had an extremely high sex drive which needed channelling, otherwise he would be in further trouble.

Mrs Hamley also told how her son often talked openly about his craving for sex when she visited him in jail. 'He explained that if he didn't get help he could see himself spending most of his life in prison. He realised he had a problem and took drugs for it in prison. He went on therapy and aversion courses. And I even went on a rape course myself to try to understand his problems. But when he was released I knew he still had them. He and I continued to discuss his sexual drive. I recall an occasion when it was said between us that if Richard had 20 girls in a day it wouldn't be enough for him.

'I can say Richard doesn't actually enjoy sex because he has told me so. It's really like a drug to him, as if he's feeding off the woman. As his mother, I pray he gets all the help he requires this time.'

Perhaps the final word on the serial sex attacker should rest with Terry Cox, who lodged with Baker's mother. Mr Cox, 67, told how Baker 'turned grey' as they all watched a television news item about the hunt for a serial rapist who was terrorising London and the South East. 'It must have mentioned DNA. Richard turned to his mum and said, "I don't understand – what is this DNA?" His mum said, "You don't need to understand it Richard."' How wrong she was.

9

THE M25 RAPIST

DNA evidence was to be the downfall of Antoni Imiela – and he knew all along it would be.

His twelve months of ferocious lust-fuelled attacks around the country left a string of brutalised young girls and women in its wake, and resulted in the largest operation to trap a sex fiend since the hunt for the Yorkshire Ripper some twenty-five years earlier. The tattooed railway maintenance worker was fully aware that the science of forensics had moved on immeasurably since the days of The Ripper. That meant, he realised, that any traces of his DNA left at crime scenes might lead to his capture. So he set about destroying the evidence by keeping the stained clothing of his victims, whose ages, shockingly, ranged from ten to 52, rather than leaving it at the scene.

Bisexual Imiela took this to such lengths that he even

managed to acquire two nicknames: one was 'The M25 Rapist', based on the initial area of his attacks, the second was 'The Trophy Rapist', due to his habit of keeping the victims' clothes. At first, this grotesque routine was seen as an example of his fixation with his victims and the items they wore, but the truth was more prosaic: he knew he could be traced from the clothes and he wanted to cover his perverted tracks. It was all to no avail. DNA was to trap him in the end, but not before he embarked on a rampage of depravity that even case-hardened detectives were horrified by.

The depths to which he sank – including gloating over a mobile phone to the mother and sister of one of his victims at the very moment he was abusing her – were truly sickening.

The story of Antoni Imiela began in Lubeck, West Germany, where he was born in 1954 to a Polish father, also Antoni, and a German mother, Elfriede. Part of his early childhood was spent in a displaced people's camp before the family moved to the UK in 1961 where, after spending time in Worthing, West Sussex, they moved to County Durham and settled in Newton Aycliffe. One day, when he was still a boy, his mother, already tiring of his behaviour, went out to get some fish and chips and never came back – she'd left home for another man. She was to die before his arrest and trial on the rape charges; perhaps that was a blessing. For consolation his father withdrew to his pigeon loft after losing his wife, spending more time with his treasured birds than with his children, although when the young Antoni misbehaved he would still be beaten with a leather belt or have his head shaved by his bullying father. Sometimes his father, also dead by the time his son was to become infamous, would even threaten to burn out his eyes with a cigarette lighter.

Years later, the fiend's younger sister Jadwiga was to say, somewhat surprisingly, 'Despite everything, Antoni and Dad were very close. But Dad had a violent temper and a cold, cruel streak in him. You knew there was a line you could not cross with him. Perhaps it runs in the family. One time, this bald kid came up to Mam in Woolworths and called out to her, but she said 'I'm not your Mam'. She did not recognise it was Toni, but Dad had shaved off all his hair as a punishment.'

At strict St John's Catholic school in nearby Bishop Auckland, Imiela was ridiculed for his distinctive German accent – a severe handicap in the North-East of the 1960s – and as he grew up he became what his family called 'a natural fighting machine', frequently playing truant and picking fights with other teenagers. To pass the time he would set fire to stray cats and dogs using lighter fuel.

He was given a fine and probation for burglary in 1970, and in May 1971 was sent to borstal for firearms offences. In February 1987 he lost his job as a plasterer and subsequently used a sawn-off shotgun to steal £10,000 cash from a crowded post office in Darlington. He then delighted in taunting the police, even telephoning the officer leading the hunt, Detective Inspector Arthur Proud. A taste of things to come, perhaps. In January 1988 Imiela drove through a roadblock of armed police on his way to see his partner and their son, passing undetected thanks to a disguise. Scared that he would be shot, he gave himself up to Mr Proud the next day.

In fact Imiela was convicted of nearly 100 offences and sentenced to a total of more than 21 years imprisonment in total, although he was to be released early from jail. His crimes included armed robbery – for which he received a 14 year sentence – burglary, assaulting a police-officer, drink-driving, theft and handling stolen goods. At no stage, however, was his DNA recorded, but more of that later.

Once, at the Iron Horse pub in his home town, he was charged with grievous bodily harm after he 'pummelled' five men he claimed threatened him, and later, while serving time for a series of post office raids, Imiela put a sign on the wall saying, 'Anybody who has a problem with me can come to my cell and have a go'.

His private life was not too pretty either. He regularly beat up his early partner Allyson Pletts, by whom he had a son, Aidan. They met when she was just 16 and he was 22. He would also boast proudly about hitting prostitutes and any man he thought might be interested in Allyson also felt the power of his fists. After splitting up with Allyson, who had earlier dated his tattoo-artist elder brother Andy, Imiela, who had moved South by this time, met bride-to-be Christine. This was in November 1996 and Christine was still married, but that marriage was rocky, and after she split with her husband, Imiela came round to see her more and more. Two weeks after her husband left he moved in with Christine and would kiss and cuddle her in front of her 14-year-old daughter Cheryl. As a prospective step-father he greeted the teenager with a cheery 'Hello Pet' and even decorated her bedroom, painting her ceiling white with blue clouds on it.

The youngster was a bridesmaid when the couple married at Ashford Register Office in Kent in September 1997, and at Christmas he bought her a sexy, gold lace dress that she'd wanted for ages.

But the writing was on the wall for Cheryl when, at the age of 16, she was getting changed in her bedroom and Imiela barged in. In later years she said:

'He'd always knocked before and I was startled. As I turned around my dressing gown fell open and he saw everything. "Oh sorry. Cup of tea?" he asked. "No thanks," I stuttered. I was embarrassed and had an uneasy feeling that he wasn't that sorry at all.

Later that evening I went down to make a coffee when suddenly Tony confronted me.

He leered at me and said: "What did you mean by that earlier?" He was obviously talking about the incident in my bedroom – he seemed to be accusing me of flirting with him. As I tried to convince him that he was mistaken, his eyes lingered over me, sending a shiver through my body. I saw something in his eyes that night that I'd never seen before and it scared the Hell out of me. His eyes bore through me and I knew exactly what he was thinking – he wanted me, he wanted sex. I couldn't sleep that night and kept going over it in my head. In the morning I felt silly.

Was I making a fuss over nothing? Then soon afterwards one of our neighbour's accused Tony of groping her. He denied it and Mum defended him. "He'd never do that," she screamed. "You just fancy him for yourself." Before I knew what I was saying, I blurted out: "He tried it on with me too." Afterwards Mum never talked to me about what I'd said. Tony had come between us and I no longer felt safe in my own home.'

She was right to feel concerned, and the neighbour in Appledore in Kent who had accused Imiela was later to play a crucial role in his capture. That woman was Kathy Sherwood. Imiela had grabbed and attempted to kiss her in her home, but she managed to fight him off. She never forgot the incident, however, and years later it was to lead to Imiela's downfall. Her crucial role in his capture lay ahead, however, when in the early 2000s, labourer Imiela became a railway maintenance engineer covering miles of track. The slack system under which he laboured was to provide him with ample time to pursue his perversions while, in theory, being hard at work.

So began his reign of terror that was to lead to that massive manhunt, a seven week trial in which his victims had to give tearful, horrific evidence, and his eventual sentencing.

The first of the attacks came on 15 November 2001, when he attacked a ten-year-old girl in Ashford, Kent, as she stood outside a youth club. After raping her he left her wearing just a sock and a T-shirt. Crucially he had also left traces which enabled his DNA profile to be obtained and, realising this, he desperately tried to hide any further traces.

His final attack came on 21 November 2002, again on a ten-year-old girl who he snatched from the street in Birmingham and took on a five-hour car-ride, during which he continually attacked her. By then, however, he knew the net was closing in on him. Neighbour Kathy Sherwood had contacted police after seeing a television e-fit image of a sex attacker being hunted by police, and the picture – together with the fact the fiend smelt heavily of tobacco – made her feel it might be Imiela, and so she had contacted the police. They had then taken a DNA sample from him. This took place just two days before the second ten-year-old was attacked.

In the year between the two attacks on little girls, his victims included same-day attacks on a 30-year-old jogger and a 26-year-old nurse, whose mother he gloatingly told on a mobile phone, 'I've just shagged your daughter'.

An attack on 25 October 2002 marked the beginning of the end for Imiela. His 14-year-old victim managed to get a good enough look at him during the attack to enable police to produce the e-fit, which, when it was shown on Crimewatch, prompted thousands of calls, including the one from Kathy Sherwood. When police called at his semi-detached home on a quiet estate in November 2002, he even had the nerve to laugh at his resemblance to the e-fit and told police, 'It's not me'. Reluctantly, he agreed to give a DNA sample saying, 'If the result is positive I'll jump out of the window when you come back to arrest me'. It took police a few days to have the sample analysed and in that brief 'window', Imiela raped for the last time, kidnapping the ten-year-old girl in Birmingham at knifepoint and subjecting her to her five-hour ordeal.

A few days later, on 2 December, one of the men leading the hunt for the rapist, Detective Superintendent Colin Murray, was telephoned and told that Imiela's DNA was a 29 billion-to-one match to the youth club attack, so he immediately set about organising an elaborate ambush. After trailing him, four police vehicles boxed Imiela in as he drove his car along a motorway shortly before midnight that evening.

Thames Valley Police said in a short, unemotional statement the next day:

'Detectives from Operation Orb, an inquiry into a linked series of rapes on girls and women across the South East, have arrested a 48-year-old man from the Ashford area of Kent. He was arrested at 11.30pm on Monday near Junction 5 of the M20. He has been taken to a police station in Kent to be interviewed.' They'd got their man!

So it was that in the middle of January 2004 prosecutor Mark Dennis outlined to a seven-man, five-woman jury at Maidstone Crown Court the events that led to Imiela being on trial. It made chilling listening as he catalogued in detail the nine rapes Imiela was charged with, but if his opening speech was dramatic enough, the evidence the jury was to hear from Imiela's victims was even more harrowing.

An early foretaste of what was to come was video evidence from the first of his two ten-year-old victims.

The terrified child cuddled a fluffy puppy toy as she told a woman officer that her attacker had said she should pretend he was her dad. She said the man spoke to her outside the youth club where she was putting up posters, before putting his hand over her mouth and taking her into secluded woodland nearby. The girl had said: 'Please don't do anything to me. I'm innocent,' to which he responded, 'Yeah, I know you are, and if you shut up I won't hurt you'. She added that he told her that if she was to 'scream or cry or anything' he would break her legs or kill her, 'so of course I stopped'. After the attack, Imiela allegedly told the girl to count to 500 while he fled.

She said: 'I was lying on the grass counting with nothing but my top I had on which had a flower on. It was lucky I was wearing it because otherwise I would have been naked.' Eventually the youngster ran towards the road to a bungalow where she said she 'knew the owners a little bit'. She added: 'I went and knocked on the door and said, "Can you help me?" I went in and they got a blanket and wrapped me up with it.'

The girl's mother, unlike her daughter, came face to face with Imiela in court.

Imiela refused to make eye contact with the woman, keeping his head down as she gave evidence. After she left the court he sat up and appeared to wipe away a tear, blowing his nose into a handkerchief. The mother told the jury that knickers found hanging from a tree near the club 'matched the white pair my daughter had at home'. She added that her daughter was so traumatised, she thought she could see her attacker four days later. 'We were driving along the road and she saw these two men crossing ahead,' the mother said. 'She said to me, "That's him," but we didn't connect at the time. It was something about this person's eyes that she connected with.'

Crucially, a forensic expert told the jury that DNA found on the girl after the attack matched Imiela's profile.

Gillian O'Boyle, of the Forensic Science Service, said the DNA profile was identical to that taken from the defendant after his arrest a year later. She said: 'The profile obtained from both sets of swabs matched Antoni Imiela. If semen had come from Antoni Imiela I would expect to find a match between the two profiles. If the semen had come from someone else unrelated to him then the chances of obtaining a match is in the order of one in one billion.'

If the little girl's story had been distressing enough, the evidence of a 30-year-old jogger who pleaded to God for her life as she was attacked by Imiela was just as blood-chilling. She was punched so many times that she almost lost consciousness. The attacker then tied her hands behind her back and raped her twice. But she was so relieved to be alive that she actually thanked him for not killing her.

The evidence from the married woman, his second victim, was read out to the court. The jogger, a clinical researcher, who described herself in the statement as slim with blue eyes and shoulder-length blonde hair, was attacked and raped in woodland at Earlswood, Surrey, while she was running home on a secluded pathway.

'In response to my struggling, he punched my face repeatedly and said, "If you scratch me I'll kill you". I tried to scream but he held my throat so tightly that only a slight noise came out. I was terrified. I didn't know what he wanted.' The court heard how the man, whom she described as having weatherworn skin and smelling of soap, stripped her naked and took off her red trainers, throwing them into the river with an over-arm motion. She said this action terrified her, adding, 'I thought, *he is not planning for me to walk away from this.* I was desperate to survive. I thought that submitting to him was the only way that I was going to avoid being killed. My mind raced with confusion. I tried thinking of something to say and I told him I was pregnant, which I am not, to try to make him stop, but it didn't. I thought, *please God, what is it going to take to stay alive? Please, let me stay alive.*'

When the man finished he tied her feet and hands together with her jogging pants and ordered her not to move for 20 minutes.

She said: 'I thanked him for letting me live. I was scared, but felt much relieved that I was still alive'. When he had fled the woman tried to shout for help but her voice was 'just a squeak'. She eventually flagged down a motorist who contacted the police and her husband.

Then, later that same day, in perhaps the most sickening of all his crimes, Imiela pounced on a 26-year-old nurse in Putney and gloated over his sordid act to the woman's mother while he was abusing her.

The victim had been trying to get fit for a sponsored walk. She said: 'I heard someone running behind me and I thought it was a jogger so I did not turn round to look. I just carried on walking, then, I felt an arm around my throat from behind. I screamed. A voice told me, "If you scream again, I will break your neck". I think he said, "I don't want to get caught again."'

She was dragged off the path to beside a fence, stripped, tied up with her own clothes and raped. Her T-shirt was put over her face so she could not identify her attacker. The young woman told police the rapist was a tanned man in his 40s, with a North-east accent, who smelt dirty.

Imiela stole the woman's mobile phone during the attack and rang her mother to say: 'You know your daughter, the blonde one... I have just shagged her.'

The victim's mother told the hushed court: 'I was stunned. I think I said, "Who is this, who are you?" He said, "Oh you will hear all about it later". Then the phone went dead. He sounded as if he was quite pleased with himself, almost bragging at what he had done. He had a northern accent, I would say a North-east accent.'

She dialled 1471 to see who had made the call and the number that came up was her daughter's mobile phone. 'I felt absolutely panic-stricken. I didn't know what to do. I panicked for a while, then I called my other daughter.' The other daughter tried to find out what had happened. She rang her sister's phone.

It was eventually answered by a man who told her: 'She is a bit tied up at the moment'.

More victims' stories shocked the court. A 52-year-old mother described how she was attacked at knife-point while walking her dog on Wimbledon Common.

She sobbed in court as she as she recalled 'He put a knife to my eyes and said, "See this?" and then he put it to my neck and said, "Feel this? It's a knife. I'm going to use it on you if you do anything like that again". He said, "If anyone sees us, they'll just think we're lovers and we've just had a lovers' tiff."'

Imiela asked if she was a virgin. 'I just said, "I'm 52". I could feel he was surprised. I thought he might let me go, but he didn't. I thought about my family. All the time I was aware that in one second, he could press the knife into my neck. I thought, "If you are going to kill me, just kill me". I'd really lost the will to live at this point. I could feel him getting agitated and angry and I thought he would take his anger out on me. He yelled at me, "Relax, relax". It seemed to go on for ever.' Afterwards, she said, he bound her feet with her bra and told her: 'Don't move for five minutes or I'll come back and slit your throat'. His final words to her were 'By the way, you weren't a bad ride'. The woman said she was so terrified that when she tried to tell two passers-by what had happened she couldn't say the word rape. 'I still can't say the word,' she added.

The second 26-year-old Imiela attacked was left naked with a bin-liner over her head in woods, after being tied up with her bra, top and pants as she walked home carrying shopping near Dorking, Surrey. After the knifepoint attack she dressed and ran into the road pleading for drivers to help.

Still the horror stories continued.

A 13-year-old girl told how she bravely argued with her attacker during the terrifying ordeal, telling him: 'You make me sick'. The teenager said she repeatedly 'stuck up for herself' after being dragged off her bicycle and assaulted by the man, while returning home from some stables in Surrey.

A video of the girl's interview with police – recorded two days after the attack – showed her holding hands tightly with her mother as she described how she was snatched in a wooded area. She said she had seen the man shortly before he pounced and described him as 'having a body like the character Phil Mitchell from East-Enders and a face like his brother Grant.'

'I gave a smile to say "Hi" and he just ignored me and kept on walking. I just totally regret that now,' the girl told the police officer interviewing her, who assured her, 'I would say never give up smiling'. The girl then described how she was suddenly grabbed off her bike, dragged into woods, pushed over and ordered to take some of her clothes off. 'He was saying, "What age are you?" and I went "Thirteen". He said: "That's a lovely age, a lovely age". I said, "Why?" and he said "You're growing".' The schoolgirl then recalled telling him: 'You make me sick'. She added: 'I said, "What are you going to do with me afterwards – am I going to be able to see my family? You're not going to kill me and stuff." He said: "No, I am not going to kill you"'. The girl said she continued to 'say things' to her attacker despite being stripped of her clothes. She was told to put her top over her head so she could not see attacker. 'I was just rejecting everything. I said, "Excuse me, I don't even know you and you're doing this to me". He was a sick man.'

The girl said that after the assault she sat for two minutes 'crying her eyes out' before finding help from a man walking his dog. 'I fell into his arms and said, "I have been raped, take me home," and started crying. His arm was around me trying to comfort me.'

Next came a 14-year-old rape victim who described how Imiela promised he only wanted to touch her. Five minutes later he said 'I've changed my mind' and subjected her to a terrifying 20-minute rape ordeal, in which he threatened to kill her. She was pulled into woods at Stevenage in Hertfordshire where the man cut off her bra and slashed the top of her jeans. 'I was scared and shaking,' she said, again in a videoed interview, 'it was hurting me and when I said it was hurting me he didn't really care. I thought I was going to die, I thought he was going to kill me and leave me there.'

Crucially the girl had a blue Primark carrier bag obtained during a shopping trip the previous day. The rapist told her, 'Let me have a look at it' and emptied the contents out. Then he put it under her head like a pillow as he raped her. Police later recovered the bag and found Imiela had left his fingerprint on it.

Imiela's final victim, again just ten-years-old, was called his 'final act of defiance' by the prosecution. The reason was simple: he had given his DNA swab two days earlier and must have realised his days of freedom were numbered. Her story, again recounted in a video interview, was possibly the most heart-rending of them all – if such a thing was possible.

The girl wept as less than 24 hours after her ordeal she recalled her five-hour tour of the Midlands – where Imiela had driven from his Kent home. It began when she was snatched from the street by a man wielding a knife. As she cried and begged for mercy, he told her: 'I've got nothing to lose but you've got your family to lose.' Wearing a blue, fleecy Winnie the Pooh top, she clasped her hands tightly as she relived her ordeal. In a clear voice, she told a woman police officer how after leaving home at 4pm to see a friend, she realised that she was being followed by a man in a car: 'He was driving slowly and I started to walk faster and he started to drive faster. I think he thought I was a boy but my hood fell down and he could see I was a girl.

He wound his window down and he said, "Do you want a lift?" and I said, "No". Then he pulled his knife out and said, "Get in the car or I will kill you"'. The girl said the weapon was a silver penknife with a three-inch blade, and throughout the journey the knife was placed next to the man's knee. He warned her that it was 'sharp', to 'scare me'. With the car's central locking system on she couldn't escape and Imiela told her to call him Tony, even though he said it wasn't his real name. He then said they were going to collect some pigeons. 'He smelt terrible, really stinky and he smelt of cigarettes,' she said.

By the time Imiela's lust was sated it was 8.35pm and dark. He made his young victim clean herself with tissues and a bottle of milk-shake to hide 'evidence'. Then he dropped her off in a Birmingham street and gave her a £10 note for a taxi home. He told her he had given other girls – one as young as eight – £100 to stop them telling their parents. The girl added: 'He said, "Don't look back. I am going to look back and if I see you doing it I will drive back and kill you'". She ran into a nearby pub and asked the landlady to call her mother who rang the police.

The DNA evidence against Imiela was already formidable and a forensic scientist, Dr Nicola Peck, told the court that tests carried out on DNA found on one of the girl's hands showed that two people's genetic material was present. She said that DNA components belonging to the girl were removed so scientists could assess the genetic material that was left. 'These remaining components matched the corresponding components of Antoni Imiela's profile. I estimated that it was 110 times more likely that the DNA originated from [the girl] and Antoni Imiela than it originated from [the girl] and a person unrelated to Antoni Imiela.' Dr Peck added that a trace of semen had also been found in a swab taken from around the girl's mouth in a medical examination carried out after the attack, and she said that three DNA components found in the sample – two of which were unconfirmed – could be found in Imiela's full profile. The scientist told the court that similar results were obtained from tests carried out on nail scrapings and clippings taken from the girl. Again, only minor components of DNA were found but she confirmed that they were present in the profile of Imiela.

The DNA evidence against Imiela was mounting. More expert evidence was produced which stated that 128 fibres from Imiela's clothes matched with those found on all but one of his victims.

When Imiela's 54-year-old wife Christine entered the

witness box she said she had been 'devastated' when police called to take DNA samples from her husband.

But what she said from the box was nowhere near as sensational as her husband's evidence. He denied all the crimes attributed to him – and tearfully announced he had been gay all his life!

Imiela said he regularly cruised gay bars and had had 'a lot of significant relationships' with men, vehemently denying the year-long campaign of rape and terror. On the day of the Birmingham attack he said he had had sex with a man in the city, and that the ten-year-old had got into the car asking for a lift home. 'She begged us to take her home as she was in a bit of bother. I said to her, "you shouldn't get into cars with people you know"… I never laid a finger on her.'

When asked for an explanation about the full DNA profile found on the first ten-year-old, who was allegedly raped in Ashford, Kent in November 2001, he once again broke down and told the jury again: 'You can hang me but I didn't hurt her'.

Imiela also told the crowded courtroom about his previous relationships with both women and men. 'I have been with a few women but my first proper being with a woman was when I was 19. But I'd been previously engaged with other things. I've been gay most of my life,' he added, choking back tears.

Mrs Rebecca Poulet QC, defending, asked: 'Did you have any significant relationship with a man?'

Imiela answered: 'I have had a lot of significant relationships. The longest was about two years between 1979 and 1981'. Imiela said he went out with a girl called

Alison for seven years, adding 'I get on well with women. I have probably had a lot of girlfriends that are friends, you know, but three or four women that I have probably stayed with'. He told the court he would travel to London to visit male prostitutes.

'I was pretty stupid. As I already told you, I'm gay. It was men. I went with a few prostitutes,' he said. 'I used to shoot up to London, Earls Court, the West End and the usual gay bars.'

When Mrs Poulet asked him if his wife knew he was gay, he said he once told her that he used to be. During cross examination Imiela agreed the attacker had cruelly tormented his victims by asking if they were virgins, and when Mr Dennis said the man had shown contempt for them, Imiela replied: 'I would say more than that'. Mr Dennis asked: 'What's more than that?' Imiela said: 'Well, he is a beast'. He even said of one of the attacks: 'Anybody who has done something like that is sick'. Imiela made a series of cocky replies as Mr Dennis pointed out that he had a lot in common with the rapist. He said: 'Where DNA is left on any of our victims it matches yours'. Imiela replied: 'So they say'.

Mr Dennis then said Imiela and the rapist were of similar age, height and appearance and were in the same areas when attacks occurred. Imiela said: 'That's why I'm standing here'. Mr Dennis said: 'You are in the unique position of having matching DNA'. Imiela merely replied: 'Pretty heavy'.

Still he maintained he had been 'well fitted up' adding 'I think the police were under quite a lot of pressure in this case, and if somebody fitted one bit of DNA they would fit them up. I'm the unusual suspect'. He even claimed that his fingerprint, which was found on a plastic bag belonging to a victim in Stevenage, had been planted by police officers, adding: 'If I'd done the bloody thing I would have pissed off out of the country.'

His protestations of innocence didn't sit too well with other evidence the jury was hearing, though. Scientist Dr James Walker, called by the defence, told the court that he had checked the results of DNA tests carried out by the Forensic Science Service in the case and had reported his findings to Imiela's defence team. He said he had been unable to make his own comparison of Imiela's DNA profile with that of the first ten-year-old's attacker as the 'crime' sample had apparently 'deteriorated' in the two years since the rape in Ashford. But under cross-examination he admitted that he had found no 'major flaws' with the work of the FSS, which he described as being to the 'highest standard'.

Mr Dennis then asked him about the 'one in one billion figure' obtained by the FSS in relation to the Ashford attack. 'It is probably in excess of hundreds of billions,' Dr Walker told the court. He also agreed that the figure suggested that only three men in the world would have DNA matching the profile of the attacker.

The trial had lasted seven weeks, but it came as no surprise when the verdicts were announced – guilty.

Mr Justice Owen handed down seven life sentences to Imiela after he was convicted of raping four women and three girls and was also given concurrent sentences of 10 years, seven years and 12 years for the kidnap, indecent assault and attempted rape of the 10-year-old girl in Birmingham.

The Judge told him: 'You have been convicted on overwhelming evidence of a horrific series of rapes and, in relation to the final victim, kidnap, indecent assault and attempted rape. You are a ruthless sexual predator who carefully selected where you could strike at your victims, overwhelming them with force or threats to kill, dragging them under the cover of undergrowth. Most thought they would die at your hands, four of your victims were young girls, two aged 10, a 13-year-old and a 14-year-old. You subjected them to humiliating and degrading sexual acts culminating in rape. In the course of your evidence in which you denied responsibility, you described the perpetrator of these horrific offences as a beast. That was an accurate description, but you were describing yourself.'

So exactly how had this 'beast' been trapped?

The hunt for the 'M25 rapist' was widely accepted to be the biggest investigation of its kind since two decades earlier when the Yorkshire Ripper was being hunted.

After the first formal linking in August 2002 of four rapes in Kent and Surrey, six different forces and hundreds of officers were involved. Operation Orb was estimated to have cost over £2 million with its expenditure on forensic work, police overtime and travel expenses. But that cost could have been far greater, as DNA profiling meant the hunt lasted for months, not years, as was the case with the Ripper.

The link between the horrific rape of the ten-year-old girl in Ashford in 2001 and three Surrey rapes in the Summer of

2002 was first spotted by a team working for the National Crime and Operations Faculty. The NCOF team who linked Imiela's rapes – called the Serious Crime Analysis Section – used powerful computer databases to compare details of murders, rapes and abductions to identify serial offenders and by July and August 2002, SCAS confirmed that there were a number of similarities between the Ashford and Surrey rapes, including the fact that clothing had been taken from almost all the victims. Another two rapes in south west London in July and early August were also considered as possibly connected.

A meeting was held between top officers from the forces involved – Kent, Surrey and the Met – after which Operation Orb was formally launched. As Imiela continued his attacks – moving eventually north of London and then to Birmingham – police made repeated appeals for information.

Reconstructions were shown on programmes such as Crimewatch, interviews with his victims were published, and detailed descriptions of the attacks were issued. That meant that by the end of the investigation nearly 10,000 calls had been received from members of the public, many of which were leads to be followed up by the Orb team.

One of the senior officers involved, Detective Superintendent Murray described Imiela as 'without exception the worst criminal I have ever dealt with'. Speaking of the ten-year-old attacked in Ashford he said: 'This young innocent little girl may have had her life destroyed by this. Everyone who saw the video was very upset, it was compelling, it was awful. I have sons, not daughters, but I visualised her being my daughter and, like everybody else, wondering how I would cope in the circumstances.'

Imiela had been released from a 14-year sentence in 1996 for a series of armed robberies and his conviction immediately re-ignited demands for a national database of convicted criminals' DNA. Mr Murray said: 'If Imiela had been on a national DNA database we would have got him straight after the first attack and the other women and girls would not have been attacked. It is a political question, but anything that helps the police would make our lives much easier. Civil liberties groups would tell you that it is not appropriate, but if he had been on a national register, we would have caught him straight away'.

A spokesman for civil rights group, Liberty, said it was not opposed to the principle of using genetic information to solve crimes, but called for a national debate before any step was taken to store more DNA. Since the database was set up in 1995, the law in relation to DNA has changed, but until shortly before Imiela's conviction it allowed police to retain DNA samples only from people charged with a criminal offence.

New powers would allow police to go a stage further and take DNA from suspects as soon as they were arrested and detained at a police station, but the Government made it clear that they had no plans to introduce a database containing DNA profiles of the entire population.

Imiela's first letter to his son Aidan from jail hinted at the truth when he wrote: 'I do not know how to say what should perhaps be said... I felt proud when I saw in the papers the confidence that you put in me, and am so sorry that I have been charged with these crimes,' he wrote. He repeatedly said he was prepared to 'do the time,' and asks his son to look after his wife Christine. To Aidan, the implications of the letters were clear. 'Without saying as much, he is admitting things that he could not discuss openly. I am reconciled to his guilt. I could live with being the son of an armed robber. He did not hurt anybody and was desperate for cash. But these crimes are totally different. These women will suffer the rest of their lives. He has made our family's lives a misery, too.'

The sentiments were echoed by the fiend's sister, Jadwiga: 'Toni is a bad man. He has become some kind of monster. Maybe he should kill himself. It would be better if he was dead – but people would say that is the easy way out. Maybe he should be castrated.'

As for Christine, she was to know more of what went on in her husband's twisted mind a month later, when he eventually confessed that he had carried out the crimes. His denials, which forced his string of victims to relive their ordeals, were clearly shown to be the lies all knew them to be when he wrote to her saying: 'This is the hardest letter I have ever had to write and should have been written long before today. I have to be honest to all and myself. Fear of what I know myself having become stopped the truth coming from my mouth. I did untold harm to others and for that I am paying more than prison could ever take from me.'

Imiela's savage upbringing, his reign of terror and the subsequent hunt and capturing of this evil incarnate, and the vital role DNA profiling played make dramatic reading. But perhaps he would still be at large were it not for the role of that next-door female neighbour he had tried to molest years earlier and who never forgot it. So once the appeals to find the dreaded M25 fiend and the ensuing photo-fits and description of the man concerned achieved nationwide publicity, the net was closing in on him. The subsequent DNA swab prompted by her action was to trap him.

'As soon as I heard he smelt of tobacco, I thought of Toni,' Kathy Sherwood said later. 'When I saw the e-fit I knew it was him. I was afraid, but I plucked up the courage and rang. I gave his name, address and what time he came in. I couldn't let women and children get hurt any longer.'

10

THE ROCHDALE
RIPPER

Rochdale in Lancashire is one of those mill towns born of the Industrial Revolution and left forlorn, dwarfed by its massive neighbour Manchester as the twentieth century grew to a close and the world moved on.

The most famous person born in this real-life Coronation Street society was the singer Gracie Fields. 'Our Gracie' became a mega-star of Britain in the Depression years of the 1930s and the crises of the Second World War. She celebrated her success by promptly moving to the Italian island of Capri, beloved of the beautiful and rich – about as far from Rochdale as you could get.

Michael Hardacre – Mickey to those who knew him – would have heard of the singer as all young children in the town did, while he was growing up on the tough Newbold estate. But her music wouldn't have appealed to him and he had too many other things to do anyway. From the age of nine he was a regular visitor to the town's police station and despite his tender years he was already experimenting with cannabis.

Through what passed for his childhood and adolescence he was in and out of young offenders' institutions for shoplifting, burglary, robbery and car crime. It was hardly surprising: he needed to do something to pay for his drug habit: £30 a day on amphetamines, £60 a day for heroin and, to round it all off, often £40 a day on ecstasy tablets. It was a deadly combination for anyone to take, and certainly for a twisted mind like Hardacre's to cope with. Between 1989 and 1998 he was arrested a staggering 108 times, including, most tellingly, when a teenage girl accused Hardacre, 13 at the time, of molesting her, but she later dropped the charge.

Perhaps that was why Hardacre, released from prison in April 2000 for robbing a pensioner of her handbag, was not classified as a suspect when, from June to September that year, the monster known as The Rochdale Ripper began to strike. In a mere three-mile radius within the town, a series of attacks – each more vicious than the one before – brought terror to the once trusting streets. His victims were women aged between 19 and 65: none were safe. In every attack he chillingly told the victim, terrified and with due reason to be, not to look at him. Then he carried on with his gruesome crimes.

As the hunt for him escalated, the townspeople tried to carry on life as normal. None more so than 65-year-old Eileen Jawczak who, as August became September, received a letter from her granddaughter, Katherine. It was the first letter the five-year-old had ever written, so who better to write to than Grannie? Mrs Jawczak, a retired primary schoolteacher less than 5ft tall, eagerly told all her family and friends of the letter and gave it pride of place on her mantelpiece.

Mrs Jawczak was a Rochdale lass through and through. She'd been born in the town in February 1935. Thirty four years later, she'd gone to a Ukrainian Club dance and there met her husband-to-be John, 14 years her senior, who had fled the ravaged Ukraine after the war ended to seek a new and better life in Britain. Together they had four children, Stephanie, Christine, Clare and Jane. Perhaps they were in her thoughts as she walked to her home in Kensington Street one night after a college reunion at a local pub. It was the last walk she was ever to take.

Hardacre's reign of terror had now reached a stage where he was totally out of control, so when he spotted the slight figure of Eileen that late summer night she was doomed. She was a mere 50 yards from her home when Hardacre forced her to the ground, stamped on her face and then, in a frenzy, strangled her with her own tights. Most sickening of all, she was partially deaf and must have failed to hear his warning to look away, so he slashed her eyes with the Stanley knife he carried during his attacks. After killing her, he took her wedding ring and her rosary beads. Eileen's cheekbones had been fractured in several places and the bones in her face were reduced to fragments. She was so badly mutilated that when police saw her poor body, some of them were reduced to tears.

Even that appalling act was not the culmination of Hardacre's violence. Two weeks later he raped a young woman after slashing her across the face and stabbing her in the back with his craft knife, saying as he stabbed her: 'I have done worse.' A passer-by who found a victim lying on the ground thought she was drunk until she moaned to him: 'He has raped me. He has cut me with a Stanley knife.' The man at first thought she was wearing a red dress but then realised it was her blood that covered her body. The victim pleaded with the man to hold her and she kept asking: 'I am not going to die, am I?' The blood was pouring from the left hand side of her face as she asked him: 'You're not going to hurt me, are you?'

The man later said: 'She was very, very frightened. When police arrived she started passing out and I thought she was going to die because her eyes were filling up with blood and she kept slipping in and out of consciousness. I was very shaken.'

Among Hardacre's other crimes were an attack on a woman walking to work on a canal bank whom he raped, robbed and beat up, and the robbery and assault of a grandmother in a town subway. But his days of terror were numbered: he was getting careless. After one attack he returned home in the early hours of the morning with blood on his clothes, face, hands and socks. He told a friend of his who was at the home, a man called Owen Parry, that he had "cut a bloke up bad" and showed him his Stanley knife before putting his clothes in the washing machine.

Later they went to a park where Hardacre said he had been

fighting but there was no sign of any injured man or any blood. As they carried on walking they came to the town centre and found an area cordoned off by police. It was the scene of another of Hardacre's attacks, his victim this time being a 19-year-old barmaid whom he had raped twice, stabbed and slashed, leaving her in a pool of blood as he took £30 off her.

A palmprint here and a bloody footprint there were among the evidence being gathered against Hardacre. But, crucially, because of the sexual nature of his attacks there were also DNA samples to be obtained from his semen.

But when he was eventually questioned by police, Hardacre was to come up with a bizarre explanation as to why there were these irrefutable traces of his being the attacker. 'I could have killed somebody, I could have robbed somebody,' he said, but then claimed he couldn't remember as he had suffered from blackouts since a failed suicide attempt some three years earlier! 'I could have been doing anything while I was gone in that way – anything from theft to murder, anything.'

But during questioning about the attack on the teenage barmaid he started to change his story midway through the telling. At first he denied all knowledge of the incident but then explained his palmprint being found by saying that he had stumbled across her body. In a desperate bid to escape justice, he went on to say: 'When I first heard about these rapes and noticed I had been blanking out at the same time I thought it could be me. I don't know if it was me who committed them all, but it could have been me who committed some of them.'

Since the suicide attempt he'd been 'blanking out' for several hours at a time, he said, and after he came to after one blackout he found himself covered in blood.

It took the seven women and five men at Manchester Crown Court less than three hours to reach their verdict. A year after his arrest, Hardacre had faced one charge of murder, four of rape, one count of grievous bodily harm, one of indecent assault and four of robbery. As he had denied the charges, many of the survivors had had to come to court and relive their ordeal before the jury could reach its decision. The verdicts of guilty were greeted with applause in the tension-filled courtroom. Some of the jury were sobbing as they heard his catalogue of crime stretching back to childhood, while some of the public screamed 'Monster!' at the young drug addict.

Sentencing Hardacre to life for the murder and a total of 146 years concurrently on the other charges, Mr Justice Sachs said: 'You have subjected wholly innocent and defenceless women to abuse and violence on a scale which is totally intolerable to decent people. This is the most horrific story this court has heard.'

Detective Chief Inspector Mike Freeman of Rochdale CID said: 'Without a doubt Michael Hardacre is the most evil and violent serial attacker of women I have come across in 21 years of policing. To see him removed from society gives immense satisfaction. Justice has been done for his victims and their families who have showed great bravery. Michael Hardacre has never shown any emotion or sorrow for these despicable offences. He is a very dangerous and evil man and a threat to females of all ages.'

As always, the true heartache lay with the bereaved family. Murdered Eileen's daughter Christine, who had been woken from her sleep at 4am that Sunday morning to be told of her mother's murder, was still struggling to tell her daughter Katherine – the sender of that letter to her grandma – what had happened. 'How can I tell her the truth?' she said. She simply told her: 'Grandma is in Heaven.'

'Seeing Katherine's letter on the mantelpiece was probably the first time everything seemed real. Mum was so proud of it.'

The family had always believed that Ukrainian John would be the first to go and had even joked about it. Heartbreakingly he had set aside a sum of money for his wife's old age. 'He's totally lost without her,' Eileen said, 'not just practical things, but in every way. It has turned his life upside down.'

Another daughter, Stephanie, added: 'They lived in this house for 39 years, they loved their home, they loved this community – and they felt safe here. This man robbed us and many other people of someone so special. It's hard to comprehend really, but we know that our lives will never be the same again.'

11

TV NEWSGIRLS AND THE PERVERT

There was a time when the television news was read by grey-haired men wearing sombre, dark suits. It was felt they gave a necessary gravitas to the woes and sorrows of the world. And then came female newsreaders.

Women like Angela Rippon and Anna Ford brought a new glamour to the day's events, a different emphasis to the tragedies and dramas that unfolded on-screen. At first there were complaints about the 'trivialisation' brought about by their presence, but those sneers quickly disappeared as more and more women appeared day and night behind the inevitable newsroom desk. But with their emergence came a new phenomenon: the individuals who became fixated with them. David Decoteau was one such man.

Many of these individuals are harmless, harbouring fantasies about the women they see on screen every day, hoping beyond hope that these female newsreaders will, in some bizarre way, one day meet them and be attracted to them. Decoteau was not harmless, however. Far from it. On Christmas Day 1996 he had brutally raped a 15-year-old girl in Northolt, West London, grabbing her while she was waiting at a bus stop and pulling her into a doorway. He was jailed for 12 years for his crime.

By 2004 Decoteau, now 42, was free to walk the streets again, and this time his targets were not just schoolgirls but some of the most famous names on television. One of them was Fiona Bruce, the attractive Oxford-educated TV journalist. Among her many credits was presenting *Crimewatch*, a role she had taken over from the murdered Jill Dando. The latter had been mysteriously shot dead on her Fulham doorstep so Bruce, who also had her two children to consider, would have been particularly aware of the dangers that stalkers can pose. As a result, in the winter of 2005, unprecedented steps were taken to protect her from Decoteau.

Bruce was not alone in her worries, though. Emily Maitlis, the *Newsnight* and *London News* anchor, was another high-profile newsgirl he was obsessed with, as he was with ITV's Nina Hossain. So intense and worrying was Decoteau's behaviour that security at Bruce's home was increased and Decoteau was banned from contacting four other women under a Sexual Offences Prevention Order. Maitlis and a 15-year-old were among them, although Bruce asked for her name to be left off the order, afraid it would give him details of her address. Decoteau was also given a blanket ban on entering certain areas of London, including going near the BBC Television Centre and Maitlis' neighbourhood.

Even so, Decoteau was considered so dangerous that he was watched constantly by the police. At the height of the fears a BBC security guard even spent a night in Bruce's kitchen. A source close to both women said at the time: 'This man is a menace to women everywhere. The danger he represents cannot be overstated. The police believe it's a matter of when, not if, he harms someone again. Fiona was so spooked she had to beef up her security at home. It was very frightening for her. She is aware that when you work in television you inevitably attract your fair share of weirdos. But it is obviously a worry to her, particularly with two young children.'

Both women were briefed by police on the way Decoteau operated and issued with photos of him. A team of specialist officers and social workers kept constant watch over him and he was encouraged to stay in his home area of Lambeth in South East London.

'He accepts he is a danger to women and has been very open about his plans,' said the same source. 'He actually told police he couldn't help himself wanting to hurt Fiona. One of his favourite ways to get close to women is to pose as a minicab driver. He needs total supervision.'

Spookily, it was the second such ordeal for Maitlis, who had already suffered a ten-year nightmare at the hands of Edward Vines, a 35-year-old Cambridge graduate, who was sentenced to four months in jail after he admitted harassing her.

But relief was at hand for the women. Nine months before his Christmas Day attack on the schoolgirl, Decoteau had carried out another terrible sex assault that was to be his downfall. Although he had escaped capture at the time, his DNA profile was now known to police and when they decided to carry out a cold-case review of an attack on a 22-year-old Ann Summers sex shop worker in the mid-1990s, the trail led straight to him. As a result, early in 2007 Decoteau found himself in the dock at Southwark Crown Court, where he denied rape, indecent assault, robbery, possessing a handgun to commit that offence, and false imprisonment.

It was during his trial that the full extent of his obsessive weirdness was revealed. He had prepared a list of sex tips for himself, the court was told, writing at one stage: 'Lovemaking could be many things: violent, sad, beautiful, passionate.' He also advised himself to avoid alcohol, being in the wrong mood and tiredness before sex. Police, who searched the probation hostel where was he was living, also retrieved further writings about rape as well as a picture of Maitlis next to his bed.

Miss Allison Hunter, prosecuting, said when he was released after serving part of the Christmas rape sentence he was kept under police surveillance and found to have an 'unhealthy fixation' with the newsreaders. As a result he was made the subject of the Sexual Offences Prevention Order.

The court then heard from the defence that while it accepted the Ann Summers store assistant was raped, they were disputing the integrity of the DNA procedure that allegedly resulted in a one in a billion match between Decoteau's profile and swabs taken at the time.

The jury heard the victim was alone when her assailant walked into one of the lingerie chain's London outlets, pretended to be a customer but then pulled out a gun, gagged her with tape, tied her hands and threatened to 'blow her brains out' if she resisted. Having stolen £1,500 from the safe, he then bound the victim's feet, blindfolded her with more tape, partially stripped her in a secluded office and then raped her.

'I remember every detail,' the victim said afterwards. 'He just walked to the back and called me over to ask about some sex toy. He sounded dodgy and I tried to walk away but he blocked my way. Then he grabbed me from behind, put his hand over my mouth and pulled out a gun. He held it to my back and said, "If you make a noise I'm going to kill you! I'll blow your brains out!"'

After pushing her into a storeroom, he tied her hands and feet with electrical cord and ordered her to open the safe. Then he taped up my mouth and eyes, dragged my tights and underwear down and performed a sex act on me. It was disgusting. Then he pushed me over a desk and raped me. Afterwards he threw me on the floor and locked me in.' Decoteau had then boldly walked out of the shop in front of customers and another assistant.

Miss Hunter said Decoteau had been arrested in connection with the attack only after a Home Office initiative to review old cases. The barrister told the court the sex tips list recovered by police also included references to

Fanny Hill, the Memoirs of a Woman of Pleasure and 'sexual acts and positions on Peruvian water pots of the pre-Colombian period'. There was also mention of 'erotic temples in India', while the final entry stated: 'Jacqueline Gold, head of Ann Summers, £155 million business'. Another sheet listed a string of web addresses, one of which had the words 'cherry girls' in its title.

Among other possessions seized from where he was living were 'scribbles', Miss Hunter said, which read in parts: 'Rape is a violent act about anger and aggression and pathologically abnormal assertions of power over the victim.' Miss Hunter added that apart from six roles of PVC tape found on the premises, police had recovered an Ann Summers flyer from his pocket, detailing a forthcoming party.

The police had also found a book called *Sexual Deviants*, Miss Hunter said. The jury were shown the text on the back of the book – inside which Decoteau had written his name – which said people interested in sexual practices 'generally considered perverse or deviant… deserve compassion rather than condemnation.'

The trial also heard that Decoteau had enjoyed writing to Maitlis from prison, and that in one conversation with a police officer he had called her his 'special lady'. In the witness box, he admitted sending Maitlis letters from his cell, saying he began watching the news 'religiously' after his girlfriend had left him in 2003. 'I was feeling very depressed and I then focused on watching the BBC evening news to keep me going in prison.' He acknowledged he 'took an interest' in Maitlis and wrote to her repeatedly.

In one letter told her, Bruce and Hossain 'to keep up the good work'.

In his evidence Decoteau admitted he had visited prostitutes in Holland, filled in an application to become a male escort and used to work the streets as a 'freelance mini-cabber', but denied he had an 'unhealthy interest in sex'. He said he talked to women in the street, but only to invite them to his evangelical Bible study group or to ask directions.

Despite his not guilty pleas, Decoteau, who spent much of the trial reading a Bible, was found guilty of all the charges against him. At the subsequent sentencing, Judge Stephen Robbins told him: 'You were convicted by a jury in this court of committing an appalling rape of this young woman. The consequences for this lady are spelled out in her victim impact statement. You tied and taped her up and then you raped her as mercilessly as you did a 15-year-old girl a few months later. You were caught, tried and convicted of that second offence and sentenced to 12 years.'

The judge told Decoteau his 'continuing behaviour' since his release two years ago 'leaves this court in no doubt you clearly represent a danger to society, namely a sexual danger to females'. Among other things he had demonstrated a 'fixation' towards a number of women 'including TV newscasters'. Not only had he 'lacked insight' into his crimes, the judge continued, but as psychological and psychiatric reports made clear, he posed a high risk of sexual re-offending. 'You have a deviant sexual interest in women and show a persistent preoccupation with sexual matters.'

It was equally apparent to those who had examined him,

the judge went on, that while he did not suffer from a treatable mental illness, he did have a marked anti-social personality disorder and was someone who appeared incapable of profiting from punishment. 'Your history therefore leaves this court to conclude the only appropriate and safe sentence in this case is one of life imprisonment.'

After explaining that a total of four concurrent life sentences would be imposed – one each for the rape, the robbery, the handgun possession and the false imprisonment – along with an eight-year-term for the indecent assault, the judge added he would have to serve a minimum of ten years before being considered for parole.

At this point the initially impassive Decoteau lost his temper, looked up at the judge and shouted: 'Fuck off you ****!'

Decoteau – and the invaluable contribution of DNA profiling – were summed up afterwards by Detective Sergeant Jackie Murphy when she said. 'David Decoteau is a dangerous sexual predator who has shown no remorse. The sentence will finally allow the victim to bring to a close this traumatic attack. The technology is such now that rapists cannot be confident they have got away with it.'

Later she spoke of her 'absolute delight' with the sentence. The officer, who received a 'peculiar' letter full of sexual innuendo from Decoteau after his conviction, said: 'This means women are a whole lot safer. He is clearly a sexual deviant with a history of sexual offending. I believe there is a very real possibility he has committed further rapes and/or sexual offences and would appeal for other women who recognise him and think they may have been a victim to come forward and contact the Met's old case review team.'

Also in court to see him sentenced was Decoteau's brave Ann Summers victim, by now a mother. She, too, acknowledged the role played by DNA profiling in solving the case when she said afterwards: 'I was in shock and felt sick but I had to give the police samples. It was horrible, but in the end it was those DNA swabs that solved the case. It's funny but I remember saying: "Even if it takes ten years he will be caught."'

12
MURDER AT
THE MILL

Of all the legacies of the Industrial Revolution that changed the face of Britain so dramatically, few can match the impact and scope of Saltaire in Yorkshire. Designated a World Heritage Site in 2001, the former mill houses one of the largest collections of works by the artist David Hockney – born nearby in Bradford – and visitors travel from all over the world to see the remarkable buildings and the houses that surround them, all the result of the vision of a remarkable man.

Two hundred years earlier Bradford was a mixture of a filth, disease and poverty. Between 1801 and 1851 its population had grown from 13,000 to 104,000 and overcrowding and child labour levels were high. More than 200 factory chimneys continually churned out black, sulphurous smoke and the stench of industrial effluent and waste materials hovered over the city. It became known as the most polluted town in England and as raw sewage was dumped into the River Beck, which provided the locals with their drinking water, there were regular outbreaks of cholera and typhoid. Life expectancy was one of the lowest in the country at just 18 years.

In 1848 Titus Salt, the head of his family wool business, became Bradford's mayor. He tried hard to persuade the council to pass a by-law that would force all factory owners in the town to use new burners with lower levels of pollution, but other factory owners were opposed to the idea and refused to accept that the smoke produced by their factories was a danger to health.

So, in 1850, Salt announced his plans to build a new industrial community at a nearby beauty spot on the banks of the River Aire, near the Leeds to Liverpool canal. Eight hundred and fifty houses were built for workers, along with a park, church, school, hospital, library and a whole range of different shops. The houses in Saltaire were far superior to those available in Bradford and other industrial towns, with fresh water piped into each home from its own 500,000-gallon reservoir. Every family had its own outside lavatory and to encourage people to keep themselves clean, Salt also arranged for public baths and washhouses to be built. When Sir Titus died in 1876 his family were horrified to discover he had given away much of his fortune, but more than 100,000 mourners paid tribute to the great benefactor at his funeral.

Like everyone who lived near Saltaire, Mary Gregson

knew of the legacy of the great man, even though he had been dead for over 100 years when, at 5.20pm on 30 August 1977, she set off to work at the mill as a cleaner. Having put her husband Bill's dinner in the oven and kissed her 11-year-old son Michael, the 38-year-old took her usual half-mile route along the canal towpath from her home in Jane Hills, Baildon. Normally she would meet her friend Susan Jackson at the end of the towpath and they'd walk to work together, but on this day she failed to turn up. Nor did she arrive at the factory later. When she failed to return home, her anxious husband Bill, 50, notified the police. He was right to be worried. The next day Mary's body was found floating nearby in the River Aire. She had been strangled and sexually attacked.

A hunt for her killer then began – one of the biggest in the area's history – and more than 11,000 people were interviewed. One important clue was the sighting of a man standing over a woman's body the night Mary – described by police as a well-respected member of the community – disappeared. He was in his mid-twenties and about 5ft 10in tall, with a long face, thin nose and lightish brown hair. He had light-coloured eyebrows, a bad complexion, and looked 'unintelligent'. But the witness who provided the information was also maddeningly vague.

One of the men police talked to was Ian Lowther, a 24-year-old labourer working on the construction of a massive office block for the Inland Revenue on the banks of the River Aire. All 800 workers on the site were quizzed and Lowther said he knew of the murder because he had seen it on television but he had never met the dead woman. Initially he said he was working at the time of Mary's disappearance, but this turned out to be untrue. That in itself was no indication of guilt, however, as many of the men on the site would skive off for a drink, and that is what he said he had been doing.

Bloodstains found on poor Mary matched Lowther's blood group, but that was no great help to detectives as they also were a match for her husband's. Even as heartbroken Bill went on television to appeal for help in tracking her killer down, there were those in the area who felt the husband might know more about the crime than he was letting on. Even the 200 fibres taken from her body did not help. They might not have come from the killer's clothes, and could easily have come from the mill where she worked or even from the river in which she was dumped.

There was no breakthrough in the case, so the killer seemed to have escaped. Four years after her death, Bill, who had never recovered from her loss, died of a heart attack, a broken man. Lowther, meanwhile, carried on his life with his wife Carol and young daughter Carmen.

As the years passed, the chances of capturing the killer seemed to recede but there was still a chance that time would be no barrier to justice. West Yorkshire Police had retained murdered Mary's clothes, with the all-important semen stains on them, waiting for an advance in forensic science to enable them to get their man. And in time that is exactly what happened.

In 1985 Single Locus Profiling (SLP) was attempted on the

stain, but this proved unsuccessful, because there was not enough DNA of sufficient quality to obtain a profile. By late 1988, police worldwide were employing the new DNA testing, so the West Yorkshire murder squad reopened the Gregson files and waited for three weeks for forensic scientists to complete their tests. Still the magic breakthrough did not come, and there was more frustration for the officers as the samples used had broken down so much they could not be matched with those taken from the local male population. Further advances in 1995 allowed a more sensitive test to be conducted, but again these tests were unsuccessful.

Then, in late 1997, a cold-case review was begun. Forensic Science Service (FSS) staff examined clothing and belongings, while tapings from the original examination were searched for foreign hairs. All Mary's clothing tested negative for possible DNA material, so a speculative 'slide' was made from the material between two areas of her underwear which had previously been cut out for earlier tests. Minute samples of sperm were found on it and it was decided to send the rest of the knickers to the specialist DNA Low Copy Number (LCN) unit to maximise the chances of obtaining a profile.

The breakthrough that detectives had been waiting for came in early 1999 with the launch of SGMplus, a system that enabled an examination of ten areas of DNA, plus deciding sex. Along with other improvements, SGMplus provided the most sensitive technique yet, enabling the production of DNA profiles from just a few cells and, crucially, from old, degraded samples. FSS scientists managed to obtain a full male profile from Mary's underwear and the hunt was on again.

As the crime was featured on BBC's *Crimewatch*, Mary's younger sister Judith Sykes also appealed for help saying: 'My family has never come to terms with Mary's death and this has been made worse by the fact that we have not known who was responsible – there are so many unanswered questions. At the time we just existed. You just go through the motions of everyday life; it is not a proper life. That goes on for a very, very long time. I must admit I feel like that now.

'Twenty-two years ago we just carried on because we had to. There was family to think about, Michael, Mary's husband Bill and my family. Life has to go on as people say, even if you don't want it to. But I just tended to walk around looking at people's faces, thinking "Do you know something?" It was just a life of torment really.

'Mary was always there for me, from day one. She walked to me to school for the first time, she was there at the school gates to pick me up. She wasn't just my big sister, she was my best friend.'

Mrs Sykes, 50, also told of the heartache Mary's husband had had to endure: 'He was totally traumatised. He used to ride up and down the canal bank on his bike questioning people. He really became a recluse. All he could think about was Michael and trying to find out who killed Mary.'

After his father's death, young Michael Gregson had gone to live with his aunt Judith. 'It has been very difficult for him. He was just 11 when Mary was killed. At 11 you have all the important years coming up and he needed his mother there, but he just didn't have her.'

Even as Judith was appealing for help, the men and women in white coats were busy. Forensic lab technician Valerie Ingram was carrying out yet more tests on Mary's clothes. 'What I saw during my testing was both shocking and exciting. I realised the case could be reactivated and with a strong chance of a conviction.'

All the information collected in 1977 was fed into a computer. Happily, as match after match proved negative, Mary's husband was one of the first men to be cleared of all guilt and the suspicion could finally be laid to rest.

Mary's murder squad now asked 3,000 men from the area to give swab samples, and travelled over 20,000 miles to track down men they had questioned two decades before. One of the men they approached again was former abattoir worker Lowther, now a grandfather of four. Eerily, he had moved to a cottage where he could look out of the window onto the river in which Mary's body had been found.

Then came the moment when the killer was identified at last. Swab 532, taken from Lowther without any protest in February 2000, was a match and at dawn on 8 April the police swooped on his home and arrested him. He showed no surprise. Detective Sergeant Gerry O'Shea said: 'Lowther never even bothered to protest his innocence. He didn't even ask why we were there. He just submitted to us.'

Before allowing himself to be handcuffed, Lowther – who had recently divorced – carefully placed his slippers side by side at his front door. This act of his obsessional tidiness was just one example of his obsessive personality, which could at times 'explode with emotion'.

It was such an explosion that had ended Mary's life that summer afternoon twenty-three years earlier. He had drunk seven pints of beer that day and when he spotted Mary walking to work he made advances to her as he emerged from the bushes that separated the river and the canal. When she rebuffed him, he punched her to the ground, raped and then strangled a woman he had never met before in his life.

In September 2000, at Sheffield Crown Court, Lowther pleaded guilty to murdering Mary. His barrister, Simon Lawler, QC, told the court: 'When the police knocked on his door, he knew it was about Mary's murder because he had seen a reconstruction on *Crimewatch* a month before. He gave a swab sample voluntarily, and must have known his secret was about to be discovered. When police called the second time, he did not seem the slightest bit surprised. He was almost relieved the burden had been lifted.'

Mr Lawler added that what Lowther had done had been totally out of character. 'It was ten minutes or so of total and brutal madness.'

Paul Worsley, QC, prosecuting, said: 'It was a particularly savage murder which involved extensive police inquiries, but all in vain. Yet the police never closed the file and their tenacity was rewarded with advances in DNA profiling. When confronted with the evidence, Lowther admitted his guilt. The saddest thing is that Mrs Gregson's husband, mother and father have died never knowing her killer would one day be caught.'

Mr Worsley added that at the time Lowther was never a prime suspect, his alibi having been that he had been collecting his son from his mother-in-law's.

Detective Chief Superintendent Brian Taylor, a detective sergeant when the enquiry was first launched and the senior investigating officer on the reopened case, said: 'For me and the rest of the original inquiry team it has solved a mystery that has always been with us for the last 23 years. As a detective looking at other cases, the question 'Could this man have killed Mary?' sometimes cropped up. Now I won't have to ask that question any longer.'

Mr Taylor said Lowther, who continued to live just a mile from the scene of the murder, had not shown any remorse or given any explanation as to why he killed Mary. 'He is a quiet man who kept himself to himself. He lived an ordered life and was meticulous in his habits. Police described him as a quiet, reserved, nice man. Since the murder in 1977 he continued a normal life as a married man until his divorce in 1999. We have not uncovered any connections between Lowther and Mary Gregson.'

The police officers who nailed Lowther were later commended by Mr Taylor and presented with their awards by West Yorkshire Chief Constable Graham Moore at police headquarters in Wakefield. The deputy senior investigating officer, Detective Inspector Chris Binns, received a Chief Constable's Commendation for his determination, hard work and single-minded application. Other members of the inquiry team received an Assistant Chief Constable's Award of Merit for their hard work, sheer determination and loyalty to the senior investigating officer. They were Detective Sergeant Gerry O'Shea, PC Don Hewitt and PC Lisa Shires, Detective Constable Con Nigel Spencer, and Lisa Dennell and Michelle Colley of the Holmes incident room staff.

Mr Taylor said the members of the team had been faced with a daunting task, but had never lost their enthusiasm. 'Through their sheer hard work and determination they found the man responsible and he is now serving a life sentence for murder,' he said.

Perhaps this remarkable case, the true grit of the police involved and the DNA breakthrough that made justice possible were all best summed up by Judge Michael Mettyear after Lowther had admitted his crime: 'Twenty-three years ago you robbed an innocent woman of her life, a husband of his wife and a child of his mother. It was a wicked and brutal murder accompanied by an indecent assault. All this loss and tragedy to satisfy a few moments' lust. Thank goodness for advances in DNA profiling, for the determination of the police and that the arm of the law is long.'

13

THE SHOE RAPIST

For more than 20 years James Lloyd had kept a dark secret. To the outside world he seemed a paragon of virtue. The 49-year-old had worked for the same printing firm since leaving school and had risen to become manager of its print works, earning £42,000 a year. He was known as a workaholic, often going in seven days a week and turning up during the fortnight the factory closed for in the summer.

Married with three children, Lloyd lived in a four-bedroom home on a new estate in the village of Thurnscoe in South Yorkshire, the type of home most people in that essentially working-class part of the North would look at with envy. But when the telephone rang one day in early 2006, he knew within moments the game was up. His secret would be a secret no more. For James Lloyd, diligent, well-respected family man and Freemason, was none other than the dreaded Shoe Rapist.

He had earned the name two decades earlier when, over a period of roughly three years, he had terrorised South Yorkshire with a series of random and increasingly violent attacks on women, after which he would always leave with one of their stiletto shoes. When the attacks stopped, the police thought the pervert carrying them out must have died or been arrested on some other charge. They had samples from four of the attacks that enabled them to profile the rapist, but no match existed with any man they had on file.

Justice was not to be denied, however, merely delayed. While Lloyd had carried on working and presenting a false image to the world, DNA forensics were progressing in leaps and bounds. The process of familial tracing – where a relative's DNA can point detectives in the direction of a criminal – had created a whole new weapon in the police armoury. That was why the telephone call meant the beginning of the end for Lloyd. His sister June had been stopped and breathalysed over an alleged drink-drive offence. As part of the procedure she had given a swab that enabled police to log her DNA record. That told them she was one of 43 men and women whose genetic fingerprint was similar to the Shoe Rapist's.

Detective Sergeant Sue Hickman was given the task of tracing close male relatives of all of them and the third door she knocked on was that of Lloyd's sister. June told the detective that her brother was approximately the age and height of the wanted man and agreed to contact him so the police could arrange to take a routine swab. June didn't know it, but she was in effect pronouncing him guilty of the long-unsolved crimes.

Not suspecting for a moment that he was in fact the rapist, June called her brother. As she told him about her conversation with police and the events that had led to it, Lloyd could practically hear the inevitable knock of the door that would mean the end of his freedom.

When Lloyd learned of the match, he phoned his father, apologised for letting him down and said that he'd raped somebody 20 years ago. Police and an ambulance were called to Lloyd's home where they found him drunk. He was planning to hang himself and had already written a suicide note. 'I knew that was coming,' he admitted to the police. 'I was a bastard 20 years ago.'

A search of his home and garage revealed a large collection of stockings, stiletto-heeled shoes and pornographic videos. More shoes, stockings and porn magazines were found in a roof void at the Dearne Valley Printers in nearby Wath, where Lloyd had worked for 30 years.

The stockings and stiletto-heeled shoes were souvenirs of his reign of terror, gathered from those unlucky enough to become his victims as they suffered increasingly violent ordeals, which progressed from threats of violence to the use of a knife. Lloyd would carefully plan every one of his attacks and was confident enough to spend a relatively long time with all of his victims, binding their hands in a similar way and stealing their property. His trademark was to take their shoes, but other items including perfume and jewellery were also stolen, although police did not release those details in the 1980s when the hunt for the Shoe Rapist was at its peak.

Lloyd's relatives were taken aback by his secret life, as were the rest of the community. He'd married his wife, Patricia, 22 years before his arrest, and by that time he'd already stopped offending. Nothing he did after saying 'I do' gave anyone an inkling of his true nature.

His brother-in-law, John Willis, said: 'It has taken everyone completely by surprise. He is such a well-respected man that it just takes your breath away. I have known him for 22 years through my sister. There was no indication about this guy, whatsoever, that he had any interest in anything other than being Mr Boring, pipe and slippers. He didn't even go out for a drink. Words fail me. If you were to paint a picture of someone who would not commit that sort of crime, it would be my brother-in-law. That part of his character was like a closed book. He was a workaholic with few outside interests.'

Lloyd's sister June, the woman inadvertently responsible for his capture, was also stunned by the revelations. 'The police came round in March this year and told me the DNA from my drink-driving charge matched that found on victims of a local rapist. They wanted to know if I had any brothers,' she said later when interviewed. 'As soon as I said I had one brother, Jimmy, they wanted to know all about him.

They asked me what his character was like. Did I get on with him? Were we close?

'I was worried about his link to the crimes but I never dreamed it could be something so serious that he'd try to kill himself over it.'

The police also asked June, whose husband Malcolm had died in 1995, if she had ever suffered any sexual abuse in her family. At first she did not reveal that James had abused her.

Only after he was charged with seven rapes did she decide to tell detectives what had really happened in her family. 'I just broke down. I'd been trying to keep everything in for so many years but now I knew I had to tell them. I said: "Yes, my brother abused me as a child." It was the first time I'd ever told anyone about it because I'd tried to bury it so deep. It was too painful. I'd thought: "If I don't tell anyone maybe I could pretend it never happened." It had weighed down on me for years.

'Once when I was eight he threw a big stone at me. I remember there was a look of evil in his eyes. He took pleasure in it. I tried to pretend he wasn't this horrible person but deep down I knew he was.'

As the two grew up, Lloyd's behaviour towards his sister became stranger. 'He used to come into my room at night and watch me undress. I was so scared of him – it was like he had a power over me.'

The police asked her if her brother had been interested in such things as stockings and suspenders. 'I felt sick. I knew he had liked them when he was younger but when I found out about the twisted way he used them on his victims it was too much to bear. But I wanted to know about the crimes, to know the full extent of what he'd done to those poor girls. When I was told how he'd tie his victims up with stockings and steal their stilettos as trophies I felt physically repulsed.'

After his marriage, however, June thought he had become a different man. 'It was like he was a different person. He was caring and hardworking, his wife Patricia loved him and he seemed to have changed. In a way I felt like I'd betrayed him with my DNA. I felt like I was sending him to prison.'

Lloyd's appearance in court was delayed until July 2006 as he'd tried to kill himself while in prison, but when he did appear at Sheffield Crown Court he pleaded guilty to raping four women and attempting to rape two others. Some of his victims were there to see him admit his crimes and one observer shouted: 'Rot in Hell!' as he left the dock.

His barrister, Peter Kelson, QC, spoke of the 'exceptional gravity' of the offences and said: 'For a campaign of rape he will be facing a long sentence.'

In September Lloyd was sentenced to life imprisonment. He was told by Judge Alan Goldsack he must serve at least 14 years in prison before becoming eligible for parole. The judge said: 'Few sexual cases are more serious than these.'

In a strange twist to the tale, the court heard that when detectives searched Lloyd's possessions, they found a series of videos of him and his wife Pat having sex. She was often tied up and appeared to be comatose. Lloyd was seen to stop what he was doing and replace his wife's stilettos if one of them fell off. But in a statement read to the court, she said she had consented to all the acts and denied her husband had drugged her. 'He has always been a good husband, good father and hardworking. I had never had any indication he had the capacity for anything like that.'

Judge Goldsack told Lloyd: 'It may be your sexual fantasies have simply been contained within the relationship. Were it to end, you may well have been tempted to carry them out with other women, giving them no choice whether to consent or not.'

Indeed, one of the strangest items found in his possession was a pamphlet called *The Perfect Victim*, a rapist's charter that described trussing up victims. It was not clear whether Lloyd wrote it himself or downloaded it from the Internet.

One of his victims, 38-year-old care assistant Justine Armstrong, waived her right to anonymity when she spoke publicly of her ordeal as he was sentenced. Mrs Armstrong was just 18 when Lloyd grabbed her from behind in Swinton, near Rotherham, in August 1986 and held a knife to her throat.

'I was desperate to get away and fought like a tiger. I was covered in cuts and strangulation marks as he attacked me. There was no one else around. I'm only 5ft 5in and slim and I was wearing three-inch heels. Although he was only a few inches taller he was very strong. He tied my hands behind my back with some stockings, put something woolly in my mouth and put a rope around my neck. He made me put my head between my knees and then roped it around my neck and knees. Struggling all the while, I managed to get my left hand free and pulled the rope from my neck and we both fell down.

'Then he sat on top of me and held my hands across my chest, put my coat over my face so that I couldn't see him, then pulled my knickers down. Then he asked my name but I gave him a false one. He also asked where I had been and I told him I'd been for a drink. He told me, "I'm going to have sexual intercourse with you." He used those exact words. And with that he raped me.

'Afterwards he took my black patent high-heel shoes. I had been doing some modelling work, and he rifled through my handbag and took the photos from the shoot of me modelling underwear. He also took my perfume and knickers. Then he told me to count to 2,000 before I left. Suddenly he was gone.'

She managed to reach her boyfriend's home, the police were called and then swabs were taken and she helped to compile a photo-fit of her attacker. Mrs Armstrong said that the rape and the fact the rapist had remained uncaught for so long had ruined her life. When she saw him in Sheffield Crown Court she said that he appeared a pathetic creature. 'I could not get my head round him being the same guy that had ruined so many years of my life. He looked like a small, frail old man. I stared at him but he wouldn't meet my gaze.'

June Lloyd deliberately did not go to court to see her brother dealt with. 'I didn't go because I don't trust my emotions around him. It brought up all my anger and rage towards him for what he did to those poor girls. I've asked myself a thousand times why James did it – and I don't have an answer.'

Detective Sergeant Sue Hickman, the officer who had interviewed June Lloyd, struck a more positive note when she hailed the improvements in forensic techniques that had led to Lloyd's arrest. 'Because of developments such as familial DNA, criminals who think they have got away with it are now looking over their shoulders. They are wondering if they are going to get the next knock. From our point of view it is fantastic to get these breakthroughs after so many years.

It makes all the slog worthwhile when you can go to victims and tell them that someone will finally be brought to justice.'

In a small irony, Hickman had, as a young officer, posed unsuccessfully as a decoy for the Shoe Rapist. She had gone out wearing stilettos and a short skirt in the Dearne Valley area around Barnsley and Rotherham where he would wait for women, often as they came home from pubs or clubs, but had not encountered him.

Richard Pinchin, manager of the forensic intelligence bureau at the Forensic Science Service, also saluted the familial process used to help track down Lloyd. 'It is a major step forward. The Lloyd case was an absolute classic and more will be cleared up in the same way. DNA evidence is as good as it gets.'

Detective Chief Superintendent John Parkinson, who headed the cold-case team in West Yorkshire, added that DNA techniques had revolutionised policing: 'I'm not suggesting we're better detectives than our colleagues from yesteryear, but we now have more tools in our box.'

There is a sad postscript to this triumph of science, however. In the spring of 2007, eight months after his conviction, three judges at the Court of Appeal reduced the specified minimum term Lloyd should serve to seven years and 263 days. It left one of his victims wondering if her ordeal after his attack had been worthwhile.

'I had to go through all the details again with the police and listen to them being read out in court. We didn't know that was going to happen so that came as a shock. I also had to tell my teenage daughter, who didn't know up until then what had happened, because I was going to be at court a lot for the case. That wasn't nice. In a way it now feels it wasn't worth it. I was given the impression he wasn't going to get out for a long, long time. I was led to believe he would do his 14-and-a-half years. He could be out in a few years.

'These were serious crimes that affected so many people. I'm gobsmacked at the decision but it doesn't surprise me. I had a feeling from the beginning he wasn't going to do long – taking into consideration his guilty pleas and the fact he was an upstanding citizen. But now I know who he is and that he's not going to be in there long, I don't feel safe. I felt safer not knowing who he was.'

She was also worried that it might deter other female victims of sex attacks. 'I think people will think: "Why bother going through all that if it isn't going to be a long enough sentence?" Don't get me wrong. I don't regret doing it because I thought he was being brought to justice. But if I'd known the outcome I don't know if I would have bothered. I'd have kept quiet. I understand now why a lot of women do that.'

14

THE BODY IN THE CHAPEL

The foundation stone for the Roman Catholic St Patrick's Church in the Anderston district of Glasgow was laid on 17 March 1896 – St Patrick's Day. It was an appropriate date because the church had come into being to provide a place of worship north of the River Clyde for the increasing number of Irish immigrants who had flooded into the area, attracted by the prospects of work and refusing to be put off by the antagonism they faced from locals who were already suffering from overcrowding and poor housing conditions, and feared the new arrivals meant job losses and wage cuts.

The demand for a large Catholic church in the area had become so great that the existing St Patrick's used since 1850 was no longer suitable. Work duly went ahead on the new church, which was built in typical imposing Victorian style and completed by June 1898. But in that sectarian city, even the same religious denomination managed to be split between themselves, and local legend has it that the native Scots worshippers had a Scottish priest consecrate the church, only for the Irish 'newcomers' to have an Irish clergyman perform the same ceremony later in the day.

Many of the worshippers in the area – tea magnate Sir Thomas Lipton and comedian Billy Connolly are among the famous men born nearby – were housed in the tenement homes for which the city is famous, but all that changed in the 1960s. A redevelopment and motorway programme saw St. Pat's – as everyone called it – almost swallowed up, and a road realignment meant that part of the main approach to the church had to be altered, making the entrance to the chapel just a few short steps from busy North Street. And it was in that chapel, the epitome of Caledonian propriety, that on Friday, 29 September 2006, the body of a missing Polish student Angelika Kluk was found dead, in a small void hardly big enough to crawl into.

A police search specialist and a forensic scientist were shown a hatch outside the confession box. Below the boards was a tiny, cramped space where Angelika was lying on her back, her legs tucked underneath and her hands tied up with cable. A cloth had been stuffed in her mouth and yellow insulating tape wound around her head so tightly that her face was badly distorted. Her shirt, vest and bra had been pushed up over her chest, exposing her breasts, and in a black bin bag beside her body, police found a knife and a white sheet saturated in blood and smeared with green paint. A sweatshirt and a torn pink towel were also covered in blood and had green paint on them. She had been stabbed 19 times.

The 'Body in the Chapel' case seemed horrific enough when details of the attack seeped out, but the subsequent hunt for the killer, his arrest and then one of the most remarkable court cases of recent years, were to reveal a story of lust, adulterous priesthood, alcoholism, and a serial sex attacker, meaning that no one would ever look at the Victorian church in the same light again. Crucial to solving the case was one of the most intriguing examples ever of DNA helping to catch and convict a monster.

Angelika and her older sister Aneta had had a strict upbringing in her home town of Skoczow in southern Poland, where they were raised by their construction worker father Wladislaw in a cramped apartment after their mother left them. Mr Kluk instilled Catholic values in his two girls and he was delighted when his younger daughter won a place at Gdansk University to study science and languages. Angelika was an innocent 21-year-old when she arrived in Edinburgh in summer 2004, to earn money as a cleaner and cloakroom attendant ahead of her first year at university in her homeland. She enjoyed the country so much that she decided to return the following summer, this time to Glasgow where she started attending Mass at St Patrick's Church. After losing the tenancy on her rented accommodation she turned to the church's priest, Father Gerry Nugent, for help. He gave her a rent-free room in the Chapel House, a small complex of single rooms in the church grounds, and employed her as a cleaner.

A man in his sixties, Father Nugent appeared to be good-hearted, devoted not only to his faith but to the homeless and those incapable of coping whom allowed to stay at the church under his 'Loaves and Fishes' scheme to help those with no roof over their heads. But behind the dog collar was a man in turmoil; he was fighting a losing battle against alcoholism and after ten years off the bottle he was drinking again. His favourite tipple was Bacardi, but recently he had turned to vodka, drunk from a teacup to hide his secret. With the Alice-in-Wonderland logic of the alcoholic who denies his problem, he felt that as he wasn't drinking Bacardi, then he 'wasn't really drinking'.

But as a priest, he had an even greater secret. He regularly had sex with women – he felt that they were chasing him and he was to say 'it takes two to tango' – and even took two vice girls from Glasgow's red-light district back to the church for what he was to call a 'sexual fumble'. He regularly visited confession to reveal his sexual transgressions, which had begun in his late twenties.

Even as the attractive young Pole was unpacking her suitcase there were rumours of an affair between the priest and a married woman, and some of his female parishioners spoke of uncomfortable encounters when they believed he was trying to seduce them. Predictably he took an immediate liking to Angelika, with her youthful smile and blonde, flowing hair. He bought her a £1,500 laptop computer and then let her use his credit card to buy clothes. The cleric was also seen pressing cash into her hand before she went on a tourist trip around Scotland and the pair would often go swimming with each other. Evenings watching television together ended with platonic goodnight kisses until one night, Father Nugent was later to tell a packed courtroom, she invited him into her bedroom and they kissed passionately. 'It led to sexual activity. I take full responsibility. It was the culmination of kissing,' he was to admit.

According to the priest they had sex 'three or four times' over the next few weeks but then he felt ashamed and put a stop to the relationship. His confession to a sexual relationship with Angelika stunned Scotland, and her shocked family refused to believe it. 'It is outrageous and untrue,' her sister Aneta said later.

In October Angelika returned to Poland, but in the summer of 2006 she came back to Scotland, to the church – and her death. She started to work as a nanny for a wealthy Russian businessman, and began a torrid affair with her employer's married chauffeur, 40-year-old Martin MacAskill. The young Pole chronicled it in the diary she kept of their relationship and her life in Glasgow.

The tragedy then unfolded rapidly as MacAskill's 36-year-old wife Anne became understandably upset over the affair, while Father Nugent grew jealous and became incensed when he found contraceptive pills in her room. So angry, in fact, that he later told a church aide he 'no longer gave a damn' about her. The rows with the priest were recorded in her diary, referring to him as a 'drunk' and a 'moron', alongside her touching mentions of her new married lover, writing on one occasion: 'I am horribly, helplessly, blindly in love with him.'

Her affair with MacAskill also caused a rift with her 28-year-old sister Aneta, who was now also working in Glasgow and living in a rented flat about a mile away. Aneta strongly disapproved of the relationship and was also concerned about her younger sister's reputation. Angelika was now wearing fashionable clothes and sometimes walked around the Chapel House wearing only a revealing red robe.

Some parishioners even speculated that she was working as an escort girl. Then there was her friendship with Kieran McLernan, a 65-year-old married sheriff (the Scottish equivalent of a magistrate) who called her his 'golf protégée' after taking her on trips to a local driving range, although there was no evidence that their friendship ever went further than that.

But unknown to everyone, the man who posed the most danger to Angelika was the church's handyman, Pat McLaughlin, who befriended the young woman after meeting her in June 2006. He even called her his 'little apprentice' as she helped him with some of his jobs. Angelika mentions him in her diary, referring to a time when he offered her a scone and another occasion when he gave her Paracetamol for a headache.

On the day before her disappearance in September, Russian student Rebecca Dordi saw the pair 'talking, laughing and giggling' as they painted a shed together. She was later to say: 'It looked as if Angelika was being flirty – not flirting but being flirty. There is a difference,' adding: 'I certainly didn't approve of some of the things that were happening. I didn't approve of her going round with hardly anything on, just a red robe. I didn't approve of the priest going off with a girl to the swimming pool in the early morning.'

On Saturday, 23 September, after painting the shed, Angelika left for a golfing lesson with Sheriff McLernan. The next day, Father Nugent saw her for the last time when he left the church to visit a female friend at around 3.45pm. Shortly after that vagrant Matthew Spark-Egan was inside the church drinking when he heard a noise 'like something being dragged'.

That evening, the priest received a phone call from MacAskill, who was worried as he was unable to contact Angelika – who was due to return to Poland and her studies on 2 October – on her mobile phone. There was still no sign of her the next day, when the increasingly concerned chauffer discovered her passport and purse in her room. Eventually, at 11 o'clock that evening, the police were called. They were be met by the priest, the chauffeur and the handyman – her ex-lover, her current lover and the man who killed her. McLaughlin admitted to the two officers who arrived that he was the last person to see her. The officers took the names and details of all three men and, initially thinking they were dealing with a straightforward missing person case, returned to the station.

When they returned to St Patrick's early on the Tuesday the handyman was nowhere to be found. He had fled to Edinburgh and caught an overnight bus south. Police, increasingly concerned for the girl's well being, began to search the church.

Four hundred miles away in the centre of London, a man

calling himself James Kelly was admitted to the National Neurology and Neurosurgery Hospital saying he was suffering from chest pains. But by now pictures of the handyman had been made public as police in Scotland searched for him, and a doctor recognised the new patient from the television news as being the hunted man. Metropolitan Police officer Alan Murray, disguised as a male nurse, confirmed his identity in the hospital and as he was arrested, the hunted man said: 'I am relieved you are here.'

The truth of the matter was that neither Kelly nor McLaughlin were his real names. He was Peter Tobin, born in Johnstone, Renfrewshire, one of eight children and a man with a criminal record going back to 1965. He had spent time in a young offenders' institution before serving jail terms for burglary, forgery and conspiracy and in 1994, while living in England, he was jailed for 14 years for a vicious sexual attack on two teenage girls. He had held them at knife-point during a 16-hour ordeal in a flat in Hampshire, forced them to swallow sedatives and then raped one of them while she was partially conscious. He had beguan sexually assaulting the second girl but stopped after his six-year-old son walked in. He was eventually caught after hiding out with a Christian community near Coventry and sent to prison.

Tobin returned to Scotland on his release in early in 2004, but police did not know where he was at the time of Angelika's murder. After discovering that he had moved out of an address in Paisley without notifying them – a condition for those on the sex offenders register – they had issued an arrest warrant in October 2005. But by then, using the false name Pat McLaughlin, he had wormed himself into the seedy world of St Patrick's – and set his sights on another young woman.

The trial that began at Edinburgh High Court in spring 2007 was to cause a sensation. The fifteen jurors, the number required for criminal cases in Scotland, heard from 50 witnesses during the 25-day hearing, including the shamed priest who spent four days giving evidence – unlike Tobin, who denied the rape and murder charges against him and who did not enter the witness box.

The most startling evidence undoubtedly came from Father Nugent, who admitted his affair with the young Pole and other women, as well as his struggle with the bottle and taking prostitutes back to the church on two separate occasions.

'It was about November 2005 when I was back drinking. I was on a real low at the time ... I didn't know what I wanted, do you know what I mean? I never even had sex with them. It was more of a sexual fumble. It was not a regular thing – it was a 'two-off', if you want to put it that way. When I did it, I did it out of drink. I was out of control. I didn't have sexual intercourse with them. I think I just wanted them for company.'

On the subject of other women he added: 'I have had several relationships but it takes two to tango. There were occasions when I wasn't wanting anything but somebody else was wanting something from me. That sounds like an excuse but I am prepared to accept I have a weakness for women. Maybe some women find priests irresistible or a challenge but it wasn't as if I was on the prowl or anything like that.

Whenever I did sin, I went to my confessor, my priest. I confessed and tried to lift myself up. All through my life I have struggled with my sexuality. I have had sexual relationships with women and I have done what a Catholic does and gone to confession.'

But more important was the evidence relating to the DNA traces discovered on poor Angelika's raped, bound and stabbed body.

Police had discovered her body stuffed into a 'crawl space' below the floor of St Patrick's. It was so well concealed that an initial search of the church failed to locate it, but eventually, late on the night of Friday, 29 September, it was found.

But officers could not remove the corpse for almost three days to allow forensic checks to be completed. It was these lengthy examinations that were to prove crucial in convicting Tobin of the murder.

Police forensic scientist Carol Weston told how she was called to St Patrick's after the body was found. She was in the tiny space for three hours collecting evidence, and also found Angelika's blood, which could have flown off a weapon, on the floor and splattered on the ceiling of the garage at St Patrick's. When she was shown a wooden table leg and asked by Dorothy Bain, prosecuting, if it could have been used to hit Angelika, she replied: 'Yes, it is consistent with that.' The court also heard that microscopic traces of Angelika's blood were found on Tobin's watch.

During a post-mortem exam a gag of yellow insulating tape and a cloth were removed from Angelika's mouth. Mrs Weston explained that tests for DNA on a fingerprint on the tape matched that of Tobin. 'The probability of the DNA profile originating from another male, unrelated to Peter Tobin, is estimated to be one in one billion.'

Mrs Weston said that cells taken from jeans found in a bin at the church also matched Tobin's DNA, and that the chance of the heavy blood-staining on the left knee coming from someone other than Angelika was one in a billion. The court also heard scientific evidence that Tobin had had sex with Angelika shortly before her death.

On the second day of her evidence Mrs Weston said samples from Father Nugent failed to link him with the murder scene, and DNA from the victim's lover McAskill, his wife Anne and five others were also negative.

The policeman who had accompanied Mrs Weston when they reached the body was PC David Thurley, a search specialist. He told the court how they were shown a hatch outside the confession box. Beneath the boards was a gap was 28 inches long and 18 inches wide with two timber beams across it. He placed two plates down the hatch to the ground so that he could crawl on them and not disturb any forensic evidence. The constable said he then put a light into the hole and lowered himself down. A green plastic sheet was lying over Angelika's body and there was a black bin bag by her head. Once those items were removed, he was able to see the body was that of a fair-haired female.

'I could clearly see the young girl had a blue-checked shirt on, a pink sleeveless vest and a black bra.' Those items of clothing had been pushed up, exposing her breasts. At that point the court was cleared as a 'disturbing' video of the trapped body was screened, after which PC Thurley was asked to describe what had been shown.

Referring to her hands, he said: 'They were over to the right with a cable tying them together – two cable ties around each wrist and a fifth cable tie linking them in the middle, like a set of handcuffs. There was yellow insulating tape around her face and mouth. It goes around her mouth and around to the back of her head. It was very tight to the extent her face was badly distorted by the tape.' He said a piece of cloth was also in her mouth and her black trousers were unbuttoned at the waist.

It was decided to remove all Angelika's clothing to preserve forensic evidence before taking the body out. That was then laid on a tarpaulin in front of the confession box for a pathologist to examine.

More tarpaulins were laid out in the church and the contents of the bin bag were then opened. As well as being saturated in blood, a white sheet had green paint all over it, which had caused it to stick together. A sweatshirt was covered in blood and also had green paint on it. A torn pink towel was also splattered with blood and green paint, and finally there was a knife and a piece of wood.

The evidence against Tobin, especially that involving his DNA and the samples taken from the fingerprint, was overwhelming and it took the jury less than three and a half hours to convict him.

Judge Lord Menzies said that the case had been the most horrific he had come across. 'In all my time in the law I have seen many bad men and I have heard evidence about many terrible crimes. But I have heard no case more terrible than this one.' Tobin, he said, had shown 'utter contempt and disdain for the life of an innocent young woman with her whole life ahead of her. You are, in my view, an evil man.' He had treated Ms Kluk, he said, like 'so much rubbish'. Tobin was sentenced to life imprisonment with a recommendation that he serve at least 21 years.

As with so many terrible cases, there was a terrible legacy for the relatives of the victim to live with. Angelika's father Wladislaw Kluk said: 'Angelika grew up a very good natured, friendly girl, who always looked on the bright side. She was a wonderful daughter. When I sleep I have bad dreams. My mind is full of thoughts about how she suffered.

'My feelings about Britain are very mixed. I remember both my daughters being very happy there. And then I remember what happened to Angelika. I cannot understand why they failed to show this monster proper justice before he killed my daughter. For me, it was like she was killed twice – first when she was murdered, then when her reputation was destroyed.

'Angelika was accused of unspeakable things she would have never done by people who did not know her as I, her family and her friends knew her. I know and will remember my daughter as the person she was. It should be a crime to talk about her as they did.'

Her sister Aneta said: 'Angelika loved people. She was genuinely interested in their lives. She really cared about what they had to say. She'd scold me if I couldn't see the good she saw in them. I would sometimes get angry but she never did. She always saw the positive. That's why when she went missing so many people knew her. They knew her by her smile. She wasn't just "the Polish girl".

'I always thought she'd marry before me and I would be changing her babies' nappies and making up stories for them. I never wanted kids myself, but I could see her as a mum. Angelika wasn't scared. She knew she would be OK because it was Scotland – not England, not London, but Scotland.

'We'd read about it. We had looked at photos and we felt at home because we are highland people as well. We come from a place with forests and hills. She knew it would be all right. I would have been too scared – but not Angelika.'

Tobin wasn't the only person to be sentenced as a result of that trial at the High Court: Father Nugent was subsequently sentenced to 100 hours community service and placed on probation for a year. The priest had failed to give full answers to a number of questions while giving evidence, and had also changed his story in three separate places. He was repeatedly warned by the judge to give clear answers, but at the end of the evidence, Lord Menzies found him in contempt by prevarication. The ruling was kept from the jury and could not be reported until the end of the trial.

Passing sentence the following week, the judge said he would normally impose jail for such an offence, but he was taking into account Father Nugent's 'outstanding history' of helping others and apparent psychiatric troubles at the time.

Nor were Tobin's troubles over. Detectives from all over Britain wanted to quiz him over a series of unsolved murders – including the infamous Bible John killings in Glasgow.

Police planned to compare Tobin's DNA with samples taken from the third victim of Bible John, who stalked Glasgow's Barrowland Ballroom in the late 1960s. Tobin, who was 21 at the time, was known to frequent city dance halls and left Glasgow shortly after the killings stopped.

DNA may also yet play a part in solving the mystery of the disappearance of 15-year-old Vicky Hamilton, last seen waiting for a bus in the West Lothian town of Bathgate as she made her way home from a night out in February 1991. Detectives were keen to interview Tobin about the matter and in June 2007 forensic scientists spent three weeks examining his former home in the town before sending samples for DNA analysis.

Like many before him – and no doubt more to come – Tobin may have further cause to regret that the secrets he had hoped to hide forever could now be uncovered by DNA.

15

THE BRICK OF DEATH

It was in the early hours of the morning of Friday, 21 March 2003 as Michael Little was driving along the M3 at Camberley in Surrey that he suffered a real-life nightmare that every motorist must dread.

Delivery driver Mr Little – 'Micky' to his friends – was a hard-working and popular figure at the Ford factory in Dagenham, East London, and had recently been awarded a certificate for 25 years' loyal service by the company. As he passed under a bridge over the motorway a brick hurtled through his windscreen, shattering the glass and hitting 53-year-old Mr Little on his chest. The shock and impact caused him to have a massive, fatal heart attack, but in an act of bravery that was later commemorated by Ford from their Detroit headquarters, he managed to manoeuvre his 44-tonne lorry onto the hard shoulder, put the hazard lights on and turn off the engine before he died. He was discovered three hours later by a police patrol car.

By that time the man who hurled the brick had long since left the scene of the crime. That man, who so carelessly and unthinkingly took Micky Little's life, was Craig Harman, a 20-year-old sports shop worker from nearby Frimley. He'd drunk at least eight pints of lager that night in five different pubs and was walking home with a friend. The pair had already unsuccessfully tried to steal a Renault Clio parked on a driveway in Camberley but when they failed to hotwire the vehicle they abandoned their attempt and instead picked up a brick each from the garden next door. Harman had cut himself and so left blood not only in the car but also on the brick he'd subsequently thrown at Mr. Little's lorry. His friend had also thrown a brick, but the sports car it was heading for had managed to swerve and avoid it.

Scientific examination of the brick had provided a mixed DNA profile of Mr Little, from Hornchurch in Essex, and one other person. A full DNA profile was obtained from blood found on the Renault Clio. Then, using Low Copy Number – a particularly sensitive technique – scientists were able to show that the partial profile from the brick matched with the full profile from the car, thus linking the two crimes. But when a check was run against the 2.35 million samples on the National DNA Database (NDNAD), no match was found as Harman had no criminal record and therefore there was no official record of his DNA. However, that did not mean the DNA did not provide some key clues to the identity of the man who threw the brick.

Analysis of the ethnic 'markers' of the profile indicated the hoodlum was a white male and details of the crime suggested he was under the age of 35. A month after the crime Surrey Police, believing the killer lived locally, a carried out DNA testing on 350 men from the surrounding area who fitted the bill and who volunteered to give samples, but again no match was found. Six months after the senseless death of Mr Little it appeared his killer might escape undetected.

It was at this stage in the enquiry that police and forensic scientists decided to use the new 'familial searching' in the hope of pinpointing a suspect by searching the NDNAD for individuals who most closely matched the unknown profile – people who might be related to the attacker.

The dictionary defines 'familial' as: 'adjective; Of, occurring in, characteristic of (members of) a family.' Given that half a person's DNA comes from the father and half from the mother, there must be a similarity in the DNA of relatives – indeed identical twins have identical DNA. Standard DNA examines ten markers but familial testing increases this to 20. On average, two unrelated people might have six or seven markers in common simply by chance. But once more than 12 out of 20 markers are matched it is very, very rare to see unrelated people with so many similarities.

In the case of the brick sample, scientists discovered 16 out of 20 similarities to a man with a criminal conviction. When he was approached, he told police of relatives living within the area of the tragic attack and within two days that led detectives to Craig Harman. Over three hours of police interviews, Harman repeatedly denied all knowledge of the attack. When told of the overwhelming DNA evidence, he finally admitted manslaughter. He had given a swab sample that had provided a perfect match to the DNA on the killer brick. The police had got their man.

So it was that on 19 April 2004, when Harman pleaded guilty to manslaughter at The Old Bailey, history was made: he became the first man ever to be convicted on the strength of DNA information obtained initially not from him, but from a relative.

Asked why he had thrown the brick, he said: 'I am not sure. It was just one of those drunken stupid moments.' Harman said he had wanted to 'annoy drivers and interfere with traffic flow.'

Prosecutor Mark Dennis said: 'Mr Little died whilst at the wheel. He was slumped forward, his right foot still against the brake.' He said that without Mr Little's courage and determination, his lorry could have gone out of control with devastating consequences.

Judge Paul Focke told Harman: 'You caused the death of a thoroughly decent man with devastating consequences for his family.' He sentenced him to six years imprisonment, the first part of it to be spent in youth custody until he reached 21.

Father-of-one Mr Little's partner Susan Norman said outside the court that he was a 'precious and special man' and added: 'Six years is nothing to taking Micky's life. It's not going to change things or bring him back, but I had hoped for longer. My attitude is life for a life.'

Talking of the breakthrough that had come in 2003 with familial testing, Jonathan Whitaker, of the UK's Forensic Science Service, which had developed the technique, said: 'It is another tool for police officers. It's really reserved for those cases where you have got a DNA profile and no match on the database. The whole idea is to keep the momentum going and identify the offender before he does anything else. This case illustrates that really, really well.'

Detective Chief Inspector Graham Hill of Surrey police, who led the investigation into the death, added: 'There is no doubt in my mind that without this groundbreaking technique this crime would have remained undetected. We had worked for six months on this investigation with no success whatsoever.'

The success of the method could open the door to solving other major crimes that have baffled investigators for years. British police have at their fingertips the world's first and largest DNA database and it is one that is set to grow even larger, as on 5 April that year police forces were given the authority to take and keep fingerprint and DNA samples from suspects once they have been arrested. Previously, samples could only be taken and kept once charges had been brought. The hope was that the new powers would enable more crimes to be solved through DNA tracing techniques such as familial searching.

Some words of caution, however, came from Sir Alec Jeffreys at the University of Leicester, the man who pioneered DNA profiling techniques. He told *New Scientist* magazine that the high score in the Harman case suggested 'quite a high level of matching'. But he added that close relations could show a 10 out of 20 point match or lower – particularly if their markers are common in the population. 'Even unrelated people start to show these sorts of matches.

If you are lucky it could give you a very strong lead straight away. If you are unlucky, you could wind up with lots of false matches.'

Sir Alec added that if familial searching were to be used more in such criminal investigations, 'this would be a compelling argument to increase the number of DNA markers used.' He added that using familial searching to track people who have never been involved with the law raises 'potentially rather thorny' civil liberty issues. For a serious crime such as Harman's, the benefits were clear, he said, but for lesser crimes the balance between an individual's civil rights and the need to identify a perpetrator may be less obvious.

However, Mr Whitaker said the new technique was compliant with the UK's Human Rights, Police and Criminal Evidence and Data Protection Acts. It could only be used for serious offences like murder or serious sexual assault and with high-level police authorisation.

One thing, though, is certain. Craig Harman's hopes of escaping justice for his terrible moment of lager-soused madness on a dark motorway bridge were dashed thanks to the remarkable breakthrough by the men in white coats.

16

MURDER ON THE WATERFRONT

The second Marquis of Bute really was a man who changed the world. The Marquis, born in Cardiff in 1793, was a member of a wealthy family who grew even richer from their investment in coal in the early 1800s. His son John, the third Marquis, was later referred to as the wealthiest man in the world and a modern descendant, Johnny Dumfries, became famous as a racing driver. But it was the second Marquis's decision to commission the first great docks on the Cardiff waterfront – not surprisingly called Bute Dock when it opened in 1839 – that quickly turned the Welsh city into one of the biggest and most prosperous coal ports in the world.

The second Marquis also built up an area near the docks that, again, bore his name: Butetown. As the century wore on, the district became a massive multi-cultural melting pot – the first mosque in Britain was built there in the middle of the century – and people from more than 50 countries had made it their home by the outbreak of the First World War in 1914. Its name may not provoke instant recognition, but the name the district came to be called does: Tiger Bay. The rough, tough heart of the docks area was the birthplace of singing diva Shirley Bassey, and although the area has been changed by regeneration, it still evokes thoughts of violence and life on the edge.

It certainly did on Sunday, 14 February 1988 – Valentine's Day – when, in a seedy flat above a betting shop at 7 James Street, a young prostitute called Lynette White was found dead. She was just 20 and had been stabbed more than 50 times. Her head and one breast had practically been severed from the body.

Four thousand front doors were knocked on by police investigating her murder, and three thousand statements were taken. It wasn't long before a group of men were arrested and in November 1990 at Swansea Crown Court – after what was then the lengthiest trial in British criminal history – Stephen Miller, 26, Tony Paris, 35, and Yusuf Abdullahi, 30, were jailed for life for her slaying. But the case became a cause celebre and after a concerted campaign protesting their innocence, the trio – now known as The Cardiff Three – were cleared by the Court of Appeal two years later as their convictions were said to be 'unsafe and unsatisfactory'.

So who had killed Lynette? The crime had been difficult enough to solve soon after it was committed but advances in DNA analysis meant that the passage of time was not the insurmountable obstacle it had once been. In fact, as the boffins' knowledge increased, so did the chances of catching the criminals.

So it was that by the summer of 1999 – 11 years after Lynette's mutilated body was found and seven years after the three men jailed for her slaying had walked free – and following a special review by Lancashire Police, South Wales Police Assistant Chief Constable Tony Rogers was able to say of the murder enquiry: 'The new test may provide us with a DNA profile from degraded evidence where earlier techniques had failed.'

A year later as the case – one of 14 unsolved murders in South Wales – was reopened he added: 'Our objective is to solve the murder of Lynette White. The new investigation will be very thorough – and it will be conducted as if the inquiry was starting today.'

The original investigators had been heavily criticised for not pursuing important leads, including not following up sightings of a bloodstained man seen sitting on steps near the vice girl's flat, a man who might well have been one of her clients. South Wales Chief Constable Tony Burden ordered the new probe to be carried by a team of 16 officers led by Detective Superintendent Kevin O'Neill, and he and Detective Inspector Brent Parry, of the major crime squad, were to take swabs of numerous men in the hunt for Lynette's killer. There were suggestions that swabs would be taken from 5,000 men, many of whom had been questioned as part of the original investigation and many of whom still lived in the area.

Tellingly, Assistant Chief Constable Rogers was able to say in January 2002: 'One particular male profile is of significant interest to the investigating team – he is believed to be directly involved in the murder. He has already been contacted and arrangements are being made to take swabs. I believe the killer lives in Cardiff Bay. Most of the men we are interested in contacting are still in the locality.'

The net was beginning to close. By 14 February – 14 years to the day since the murder – police were able to say that a number of people had contacted the incident team with new information and detectives were following up those lines of inquiry. Detective Superintendent Kevin O'Neill said: 'On the anniversary of this horrific murder, we are again asking people who may have information to contact the incident team. We know there were people who were lawfully at Lynette's flat at around the time she was killed who need to be eliminated from the inquiry. We are urging them to come forward and contact the incident room. The screening process is entirely confidential.'

The process may have been confidential, but one public announcement came as a relief to The Cardiff Three and to two other men – John and Ronnie Actie – who had originally been charged over the murder but then acquitted after spending two years in custody. All five had voluntarily given DNA samples to the police and testing showed no matches with the DNA profiles obtained from the scene of the murder. A South Wales Police spokeswoman added: 'The investigation team is continuing to make progress and it is important to identify that DNA is only one line of inquiry within a number of avenues being pursued to identify the offender or offenders.'

By the winter of 2002 detectives were confident that a male DNA profile retrieved from the flat was the key to unravelling the murder. They were still taking voluntary buccal (cheek) swabs, and by that time more than 200 had been collected. Detective Superintendent O'Neill said: 'We are aware that in the weeks leading up to the murder Lynette White was frequently using Flat 1, 7 James Street. We need anyone who did visit the scene with her to contact us. As a result of DNA evidence now available we can quickly eliminate people from the enquiry and any information provided to us will be treated in a confidential manner.'

By the eve of the 15th anniversary of Lynette's death, the number of men swabbed had risen to 300 and on 1 March 2003, a spokeswoman for South Wales Police said: 'Police have arrested a 38-year-old man from the Rhondda Cynon Taf area on suspicion of the murder of Lynette White. The man was arrested yesterday evening and taken to hospital where he remains.'

What the police did not say was that, at last, they knew they had their target – a man they had dubbed 'The Cellophane Man' after the blood samples found on a cigarette packet wrapper in Lynette's flat. He had made a dramatic confession as he was being driven to hospital from his home in Llanharan after unsuccessfully trying to kill himself.

The full story emerged only in July 2003 when 38-year-old security guard Jeffrey Gafoor stood in the dock at Cardiff Crown Court and admitted murdering Lynette. It was the first time in British criminal history that a man was convicted of a murder that others had previously been jailed for, even though they were later freed.

For 15 years Gafoor, a friendless loner who emerged from his bedsit only to go to his lonely job at night or to scour car boot sales for bric-a-brac by day, had kept his secret, but the DNA trail led to him confessing his crime. He had never been convicted of any crime that would place him on the national DNA database, but he was trapped because his teenage nephew was listed.

Among the first clues police examined three years earlier when they reopened the case, was a tiny speck of blood on that cellophane wrapper at the murder scene that did not come from the murdered girl. Having found another speck of blood low down on the wall missed in subsequent repainting, detectives removed the skirting board and in a remarkable piece of painstaking work, stripped back the paint layer by layer. Beneath it they found more bloodstains from which they were able to recover further traces of blood that produced a perfect DNA profile.

This genetic fingerprint of the killer was then fed into the National DNA Database, which, although failing to produce a single perfect match, came up with the names of 600 people whose DNA was close enough to warrant further investigation.

Detectives concentrated on those with a close link to Cardiff and South Wales. The best match they could come up with belonged to Philip Murphy, a teenager who had been convicted of a relatively minor car crime. But detectives knew he could not be the killer for a very simple reason: he was just 15 and had not been born when Lynette was murdered.

They then began to interview every one of the boy's closest male relatives, including his uncle – bespectacled, Bible-reading Jeffrey Gafoor. To their surprise he admitted having had sex with Lynette a week before her murder. He told detectives: 'I thought you'd got her killers.'

While swabs taken from the inside of Gafoor's mouth were sent for forensic examination, police kept him under surveillance. On one shopping expedition the only thing he bought was four packets of Paracetamol, so after he'd returned home, they broke into his house that evening and found him in the bedroom getting ready for bed – and that he had swallowed all 64 tablets. Their quick action saved his life, although he showed no gratitude. As he was taken to The Princess of Wales Hospital in Bridgend by ambulance he confessed to his crime. He told the officers: 'Just for the record, I did kill Lynette White. I've been waiting for this for 15 years. Whatever happens to me I deserve. I sincerely hope I die.'

Later he told officers at the hospital, 'I might as well face the music. I did kill someone. I would rather not die. I must face the music. It might be my last two days on earth. I'm quite looking forward to death, to find out if God exists or the Devil.'

The reason for the murder was sordid yet sadly trivial. Gafoor had said he killed Lynette after he had given her £30 for sex but then, before they undressed, changed his mind and she refused to give his money back. As the gruesome details of Lynette's injuries were read to the court, several members of her family walked out, clearly distressed.

Patrick Harrington QC, for the prosecution, said Lynette had had her throat slit from one ear to the other side of her jaw, severing her jugular artery. 'He didn't simply kill: he acted in a barbaric manner, stabbing and cutting over 50 times, cutting her throat, slashing her wrists, cutting, stabbing and slashing her face, arms and especially the torso. It's possible he acted in a frenzy but the pattern of the injuries, especially to the breasts, suggested that it took a certain mindset. He then carried on living the same boring life, continuing to be a loner.'

The court was also told that Gafoor's sister Brinda noticed no change in her brother after February 1988, and according to Gafoor's father he seemed happy, content and worked hard. 'By that time he was carrying with him the guilty secret of what he'd done,' said Mr Harrington.

John Charles Rees QC, for Gafoor, said the murder had not been premeditated or a sexual one. 'He had a knife with him for two reasons. Firstly, in general terms the docks area was a fairly dangerous place to go at night and he had it for protection. Secondly, he had been robbed some months before by some prostitutes in the Butetown area. In the course of the argument he took out the knife and threatened her with it, in an attempt to get his money back. She refused, in fact, she grabbed hold of the knife, there was a struggle during the course of which she was stabbed.

Mr Rees said Gafoor did not know what happened next.

He knew he had carried out a frenzied attack but did not know why. It was a combination of emotions including 'shame and panic', said Mr Rees. 'He is very sorry for the killing of Lynette White, taking such a young life, and very sorry for the hurt caused to the family and the five men who were falsely accused of her murder,' he added.

The judge, Mr Justice Royce, told Gafoor: 'You ended a young life in a most terrible and vicious fashion. For 15 years, you kept your guilty secret and evaded justice, even while others were tried for a murder that you knew they did not commit.' He then praised the 'extremely high quality' of the detective work that had led to Gafoor's conviction.

Chief Superintendent Wynne Phillips, the head of South Wales Police serious crimes squad, said: 'There was a lot of evidence still in the flat and not only were they able to get a DNA profile, it was a good profile. Without DNA the only way they could have got a conviction would be Gafoor walking into a police station to confess, 'I killed Lynette White'. Jeffrey Gafoor's DNA was sent away on a Wednesday and on the Friday morning the lab rang to say they had a perfect match. It was one of the best moments of my police career. We had our man.'

The story was taken up by one of the other officers in the case, Detective Constable Paul Williams, who managed to trace a path to Gafoor. DC Williams, praised by a judge for his detective work, said: 'I haven't a clue about DNA, but I knew it worked on numbers. I sat down with sheets and sheets of names with DNA types printed off a computer. It emerged that component number 27, part of the killer's profile, was the rarest and I ran it through a search. After hours of work, I found the closest match belonged to a teenage boy who was on our records. At that point we believed the killer came from his family.'

After his conviction, a full portrait of Gafoor emerged: a classic example of a killer-in-waiting. Gafoor, of Indian-Welsh descent and one of five children, had always been a loner with few friends at school and none whatsoever in adult life.

At the age of 17 he joined a youth opportunity programme in Butetown, where he would have become aware of the call-girls who famously worked the area. When he murdered Lynette he was only 22 and living and working at the family home, a grocer's shop, in Malefant Street, Cathays. He rarely went out and spent most of his time working, watching television or reading.

On St Valentine's Day, 1988, he met Lynette, a well-known local prostitute, and ended up with her in the James Street flat where she met her fate. Soon after slashing Lynette to death he started a martial arts course but gave it up after a few months. He must have simply buried the guilt as The Cardiff Three were wrongly convicted in 1990 and sent to prison for life, but in 1991 he had gone to work in Germany with his brother-in-law.

He had never had a girlfriend and would get very offended and annoyed by pornography, which he was often teased about. Two years later, after the death of his mother, he left home and lost contact with his family. By this time he was working as a security guard, often doing 12-hour shifts and the unsociable nature of the job gave him the solitude he seemed to enjoy. That solitude ended with a knock on the door by the Welsh police.

One of the men wrongly found guilty of the murder, Tony Paris, said: 'He is evil – evil for what he did to Lynette White and evil for what he did to us. Life should mean life. I want to see him spend the rest of his life behind bars for what he has done. He watched and allowed us to go to jail knowing what he had done. He is a horrible person and deserves everything he gets – he has destroyed us all. He should stay and die in jail for the years he took away from me and my family.

'It's sad that it's taken 15 years to rectify a wrong which should never have happened. The police should have done their job properly in the first place. Instead, they destroyed me and my family. People still had doubts that we did this murder – now they know we didn't. I'm not over it yet. I don't think I will ever get over it. I will never get back the time I spent in prison. I want an apology. The guy who went down, I don't care about him. I don't know him and don't want to know him.'

The last words go to Lynette's half-sister, Kyra: 'Words cannot express the impact that Lyn's death has had on my family and the torment we have been through over the past 15 years. I miss Lyn every day. I believe that without the hard work and dedication by the current investigation team this day would never have happened. I would like to thank them for their support. Finally my sister can rest in peace.'

17

THE CROSS-DRESSING KILLER

It was a Friday night in late August 2000 in an ordinary English town when young Heather Tell set out to meet a friend to spend the evening in that most ordinary of ways: watching a movie at the local cinema. Heather, with her straight, long blonde hair, was wearing a typical teenager's outfit of black trousers, a pink sleeveless T-shirt, blue denim jacket and blue trainers with white flashes. Her father Peter, a self-employed printer, offered to drive her to the rendezvous but she said 'no' as she knew he had an appointment. Anyway, she told him, she'd be all right to walk.

Heather, just a few weeks from her 18th birthday, left her home in the Stonydelph area of Tamworth at 8pm. She was due to meet her friend Laura Ravenhill outside the nearby Belgrave Dance Studio, where she sometimes took lessons, and then they were to walk to the ten-screen UCI cinema complex in the town centre. She was due to link up with Laura between 8.30pm and 8.45pm but failed to arrive and her anxious friend raised the alarm.

It wasn't until the next day, just after 11am on the Saturday, that Heather was found, just a hundred yards from the arranged meeting place. Her body was in the undergrowth off a footpath leading from a park down towards the busy A5. The police had been contacted by her worried family – she lived with her father and elder sister Hollie as her parents had recently separated – and a hunt was begun for her, using dogs and a helicopter. The tragic discovery was made by a 17-year-old boy, one of the locals involved in trying to find Heather.

One of the first reactions of police was to appeal to the teenagers who had been nearby in Kettlebrook Linea Park. Detective Superintendent John Moss of Staffordshire Police said: 'We are aware a lot of young people congregated in the park throughout the last few nights, holding parties following their GCSE results. We are appealing to those young people to contact us if they saw Heather or anyone acting in an unusual manner, or whose behaviour now gives them cause for concern.'

The murdered girl's distraught mother, Mrs Karen Tell, said: 'She was very caring and considerate. She was always a happy, smiling girl who always, without reservation, put others before herself. Her whole life was dancing. She absolutely lived for it. It was all she wanted to do ever since she was a little girl.'

The local community in Tamworth, near Birmingham, was

stunned by the senseless murder of the blue-eyed girl who had lived all her life in the area. Bouquets, cards and messages appeared near the murder spot and a weeping willow on the banks of a duck pond turned into a shrine as dozens of friends left floral tributes and poems. A bouquet and card from her parents read: 'You were the perfect daughter any parents could wish for. We were fortunate to be those parents and we are thoroughly heartbroken.' The card bore 17 kisses – one for each year of Heather's life.

Lifelong friend Darren Byrne, 17, said: 'We grew up together from when we were five or six years old, so you can imagine I'm devastated. She was a really kind girl, she would never hurt a soul.' Close friends Shelley Barker and Hayley Gouldingay, both 17, said they were struggling to come to terms with what had happened. Shelley said: 'She was a smiley, confident person – such a good friend to everyone. Words can hardly describe her. She was a beautiful, inspirational person. Always there if you needed a friend or someone to talk to.'

As details of Heather's young life became public, her loss became even more saddening. She had started dancing when she was just four. Her former teacher at the Belgrave Dance Studio, Tracey Archer, said she was certain Heather had the ability and dedication to forge a career in showbusiness. 'She was a golden child. She would have gone all the way. Heather talked about working on cruise ships but she could have done anything she wanted.'

In her spare time Heather had worked with the Tamworth Academy of Dance and Birmingham's Dance Exchange, where she specialised in jazz and tap dancing. Dawn Haig, principal of the 150-pupil Tamworth Academy, said: 'Heather was very talented. She would definitely have made it. I think she would have gone on to the West End. She was such a striking girl, always smiling. She just had what it takes.

'With Heather, everything came from her love of dancing. No one was pushing her. She did it all for herself. She was so well liked by everyone here. Her enthusiasm for life rubbed off on all of us.'

In due course Staffordshire Police revealed Heather had died from suffocation and more than 50 officers made it a priority to trace her movements from leaving home to go to the park. House-to-house inquiries began in an attempt to pinpoint which of a maze of footpaths or cycle-ways she had chosen as her route.

The officer leading the murder enquiry, Detective Chief Inspector Peter Hall, said it was still too early to say whether Heather had been sexually assaulted and would not say exactly how she had been asphyxiated. But he did say: 'Part of our inquiry has focused on previous reports of indecent exposure and unwelcome approaches to women in this area. Over the past 14 months there have been some 50 indecent exposures reported in the Tamworth area and we are looking at these reports very carefully to see if there could be any possible connection with this case.'

He also revealed that they had received reports of someone acting strangely around the time Heather was in the park. The possibility that the killer was local to the area and familiar with the park could not be discounted, and if that was the case he must be known to people living locally. 'There may be someone who, for reasons of misguided loyalty, is shielding someone they have suspicions about. I would urge that person to examine their conscience and contact the incident room. I would hate to think that anyone could look at a photograph of this gentle and kind-hearted teenager and knowingly harbour her killer,' he added.

More than a hundred calls were received within days. The police interviewed two young men who had been spotted near where her body was discovered, but then ruled them out of their enquiries.

The hunt took a dramatic turn, however, some three weeks after the murder. A cyclist had seen a man climbing up a bank from a culvert under a bridge near the park on the night of her death. The e-fit picture his description helped to create, aided by its appearance on *Crimewatch UK*, prompted more than 50 calls from the public.

Detective Chief Inspector Hall said: 'We are delighted with the response and much of the information we received confirmed details we already had. But we have had more than one caller ringing to identify the man seen near the bridge. The television appeal has also given us one or two new leads, which we will be investigating. I am very optimistic that with the public's help we will trace this man soon.' He would not say whether the calls had revealed that the man was local.

New witness information also put the police on the trail of a man wearing dark track-suit bottoms and a white T-shirt, who had been seen sprinting away from the area where the teenager's body was found. Detectives now tried to work out

whether the runner, seen heading towards the old A5 at
Tamworth, was the same man the cyclist spotted climbing
from a culvert near the murder scene.

Friday, 15 September 2000 was to have been Heather's
18th birthday, her coming of age. Her parents had had
planned a big party at the Snowdome in Tamworth but
instead it was a day of indescribable sadness. The Tells paid
tribute to their daughter by creating a memorial garden made
up of 18 heather plants – one for each year of her life – at the
family home.

As the date passed, the parents spoke of their ordeal, a
story to break the hearts of any parents. Mr Tell said his
daughter had insisted on walking to meet her friend on the
night she died. 'We normally drove our daughters wherever
they wanted to go, but that night Heather insisted on
walking because I had an appointment. I didn't want Heather
to walk, but she told me: "You worry too much." Heather
never came home to us because some evil person destroyed
her life. So many celebrations like Christmas and birthdays
will now be marred because Heather is not here.'

Two weeks later Detective Chief Inspector Hall revealed
for the first time that Heather had been strangled and that
her body was unclothed when it was found. 'Because of
Heather's unclothed state, there are clear indications of a
sexual motive for this murder. Beyond that I am not prepared
to publicly speculate.'

He warned the worried women of Tamworth that none of
them was safe while the killer was at large. 'A lapse of several
weeks can allow the horror of this crime to fade in people's

minds,' he said. 'But I must repeat my earlier warning to women to exercise extreme caution and not walk alone in secluded areas.'

The announcement that everybody had longed to hear came on 5 October. In a brief statement Staffordshire Police announced: 'Detectives investigating Heather's murder have this morning arrested a man. The 44-year-old man was arrested at his home in Tamworth at six o'clock. He has been arrested on suspicion of murder and will be interviewed at Burton-on-Trent.'

Poignantly, the next day saw Heather's funeral and Tamworth came to a halt as hundreds of people lined the funeral route from her home to St Editha's church in the town centre. Her father and sister helped to take her to the church in a glass coach pulled by two horses, and a favourite family photograph was displayed beside the coffin with the word 'Angel' spelled out in flowers. The white coffin was taken into church to the sounds of 'Dancing Queen' by Abba.

At the service her mother Karen told the crowded the congregation of friends and relatives: 'We thank our lucky stars we were fortunate enough to have you as our daughter. We loved watching you dance and miss you so much. Thank you for all the wonderful memories. I bet you're now dancing with the angels.'

Heather's sister, Hollie, broke down in tears and in a soft voice said: 'I'll miss you more than I can say.'

Mr Tell said his daughter had been caring, loving, gentle, hopeful and respectful and always had a smile on her face. 'Nothing was too much trouble for you. You would do anything for anybody to make them feel better. That's my little girl. I don't do everything right all the time but I know for sure that one thing I did get right was you. I was so proud to be your Dad.'

The hour-long service also included a song called 'Such a Pretty Face', specially composed and performed a cappella by Heather's friends, in memory of her love of dancing. It included the line: 'I bet you're up there now, teaching angels how to dance.' Her coffin was then led out to one of her favourite tunes, 'Sunchyme' by Dario G, for burial at Wilnecote cemetery.

Hours after the service ended, police announced they had charged the 44-year-old man with her murder and he was to appear at Burton-upon-Trent magistrates court the next morning. Michael Chidgey, short-haired and unshaven in a blue sweatshirt and grey trousers, appeared in court on 7 October handcuffed to a prison officer. He said nothing during the hearing other than to confirm his name, age and address in Belgrave, Tamworth. He was charged with murdering Heather between 25 and 26 August and remanded in custody.

Heather's father and sister were in court to see him further remanded the following week, but in the interim police had been busy searching a rubbish tip at Frampton in Gloucestershire, 100 miles from the murder scene, for the dead girl's missing clothes. Mr Tell and his daughter were in court again when, the following March, Chidgey appeared at Stafford Crown Court and he denied murdering Heather. The court was told that the case would therefore have to go to a trial.

On the first day of the case, at Stafford Crown Court in November 2001, the eight-man, four-woman jury listened in horrified silence as John Saunders QC, prosecuting, told how Heather had been murdered even as she tried to use her mobile telephone to call her father. Her attacker had strangled her with laces taken from her trainers. She was stripped naked, except for her socks, and her underwear had been forced into her mouth like a gag. Crucially, the court was told, DNA samples had been taken from Heather's body and these showed the chance of her killer being anyone other than Michael Chidgey were one in 70 million. The stranger's only motivation, Mr Saunders said, seemed to have been some form of sexual satisfaction.

Secondly, Mr Saunders said, a member of the public had come forward saying he had seen a person twice that night close to the scene acting in a suspicious manner. He had attended an identification parade and identified Michael Chidgey as the man he had seen. Thirdly, at the time the killing took place Chidgey had gone missing. At the time of the attack on Heather Tell he was living close to the area where she died and this was within walking distance.

Mr Saunders continued by saying Chidgey had failed to turn up at work on the evening of 24 August, the day before the killing. 'He did not reappear at his home until the morning of 26 August. He went missing from his home the day before the killing and until the day after. He later told the police that during that period of time he had been walking along a canal towpath in Tamworth area and living rough for that period of time and saw nobody he knew.'

Chidgey had then gone to the Bristol area and disposed of clothing. 'He disposed of it,' Mr Saunders said, 'because it might lead to the awful crime he committed.'

Mr Saunders told the court that Heather had had to walk through an area of Kettlebrook Linear Park to reach her rendezvous. 'As she did so she was attacked by someone leaping out of some bushes at her. She was wearing a pendant around her neck and part of it was found close to the pathway. She was also carrying a mobile phone. We know that at 8.41pm, according to the time on her phone, she was attempting to ring her father, Peter. A button on the phone had been pushed but did not connect with the network, maybe because it was being pulled off her and hurled away and thereafter broke in two. She was trying to call him for help but that call was never connected.'

The jury then heard from the member of the public who said he saw a man acting suspiciously on two occasions on the night of her murder. Johannes Wilhelm Prinz told the court he had seen a man in the park hiding in bushes near a bridge over the A5 road at about 7.45pm as he cycled to a friend's home. He said the man, wearing a blue T-shirt and tracksuit bottoms with two stripes on the side, had hidden his face with his hand as he approached.

On his return home in the dark at about 9.30pm, he said he saw a man wearing dark clothing running near the Belgrave Dance Studio. 'I had just passed the dance studio when I heard something metallic and thought that something had fallen from the bike. I looked up again and there was a man standing right in front of me. I had to slam on the brakes to avoid hitting him.'

Asked by Mr Saunders if he recognised the man, Mr Prinz replied: 'Yes. The man I had seen previously on the way down.'

The cyclist, whose grandparents were German, said he had shouted 'Dummkopf!' [idiot] at the man and continued home. He said he'd been told about the murder by police on the Saturday evening as he rode through the park, and had denied that he had been there the night before. He said he had informed detectives two days later of the man he had twice seen there. In October he had picked out Michael Chidgey at a police identification parade and said he was in 'no doubt' he saw him in Kettlebrook Linear Park on the night of Heather's death.

Asked by defence counsel David Crigman, QC, why he had lied to the police about not being in the park on the Friday evening, Mr Prinz said it was out of 'shock'.

Mr Crigman also challenged him on the times of the sightings and what he saw. Mr Prinz admitted that although he had told police in witness statements he could see the man's socks and shoes when he was standing in the bushes, he said in court that they were hidden by grass. Mr Crigman stated that apparent contradictions in Prinz's witness statements to police meant that his recollections were 'full of the opportunity for error'.

Detective Sergeant John Bloor, of Tamworth Police, then testified that Chidgey had told him he went for a walk on Thursday, 24 August, instead of starting his 4pm shift as a driver at the coach firm he worked for in Henley-in-Arden, Warwickshire. He walked about five miles to a pub formerly called The Chequers – now the Tame Otter – before sleeping under a bridge. He said he woke up in the dark and began walking home, but spent the rest of the night under another bridge.

Next day, he reversed his route, staying at the side of the canal all day and then spending a second night outdoors, despite heavy rain. Mr Bloor told the court: 'I inquired with him how anyone could sleep under a hedge in such heavy rain. He told me he was a hard character and that the rain did not bother him.'

Chidgey said he had returned home on the Saturday morning and 'did not say much' when his ex-wife Linda, with whom he was still living, told him about Heather Tell's death. He had then slept the whole day before heading to the West Country and disposing of the clothes he had been wearing on the towpath in a bin at Michaelwood service station on the M5 in Gloucestershire.

Mr Bloor also told the court that Chidgey then came up with a remarkable reason why his DNA had been found on Heather – his liking for wearing women's clothes. He said it must have reached her clothing when he'd handled ladies underwear in shops.

In his testimony, Chidgey told the court he had left his home on Thursday, 24 August – the day before Heather's death – and did not return until the Saturday morning. He said he had left home to 'clear things in my head about my marriage and debts'. Chidgey said it was his habit to roam the canals near Tamworth whenever he was feeling depressed. That night, he had slept in bushes close to the bridge near the Old Tamworth Road, about three miles from the murder scene.

'I went to the Hopwas [near Tamworth] and sat down for a few hours. I was still feeling low and decided not to go to work,' he said. 'I found myself somewhere to sit and lie down and this time it was under a hedge. On Friday, 25 August when I woke I started to walk again. I was still feeling low and I did not want to go home because I was not prepared to have a row.'

Chidgey said he had eventually returned home, his clothes wet from the rain, before going to bed for the rest of the day and deciding to leave for good the following day. His intention was to go to find work and live in Plymouth, where he was born and spent his early childhood, but he had only got as far as Taunton, Somerset. He said he thrown out the clothes he had been wearing on his 'walkabout' at Michaelwood because of the smell.

David Crigman, defending, told Chidgey that a witness, Johannes Prinz, had seen a man near where Heather's body was found and had pointed to Chidgey on an identification parade as being that man.

Chidgey replied: 'No, it was not me. I was not in that location on the Friday night.'

Telling the jury of his interest in women's underwear, he said: 'I would visit shops and go into the ladies' lingerie department and look at the lingerie. I would be in the stores for about half an hour. It was not an embarrassment to me but talking about it is. I bought bras, pants, suspender belts, stockings and basques occasionally. I liked the feel of the material, the silkiness next to my skin.'

Mr Saunders said DNA found on Heather showed there

was one chance in 70 million that it could have been anyone other than the accused.

Chidgey, who said he had agreed to provide a sample of DNA for analysis 'because I had nothing to hide', said his DNA had found its way onto her clothes because he might have touched the bra the 17-year-old was wearing when she was killed, before she had bought it. He said he would buy items from shops like Marks & Spencer in Sutton Coldfield, around once a month.

Asked by the judge, Mr Justice Poole, why he hadn't mentioned this in his interview with police, Chidgey said that it hadn't occurred to him at the time.

Mr Crigman then asked: 'Did you kill Heather Tell?'

Chidgey replied: 'I did not kill Heather Tell.'

In his summing up, Mr Saunders said: 'What is the chance of someone else with the same DNA of Michael Chidgey not only being in the same country and Staffordshire but being in Tamworth at the time of the killing of Heather Tell, within a couple of miles of a man with this DNA?'

The jury agreed and at the end of the ten-day trial found him guilty by an 11-1 majority. Heather's father, Peter, and her sister, Hollie, held hands and hugged as the verdict was announced. The teenager's friends, many wearing sprigs of heather in her memory, cheered and applauded from the packed public gallery.

The jury then heard of Chidgey's history of crime and sexual perversion. He had first come to the attention of the police in 1971, when he was given a conditional discharge after being arrested for indecent exposure at the age of 16. A string of indecent exposure cases had followed, with nine convictions between 1972 and 1974. One of these offences was committed in Belgrave Park where, 27 years later, he was to murder Heather. He had been fined £25 with £20 costs and told by a magistrate: 'We have a duty to protect young women walking the footpaths and public places from people like you. Our advice to you is to grow up and the sooner you take that advice to heart, the better.'

But Chidgey took no heed of this warning. At Birmingham Court in 1983, he was convicted of a serious sex assault after approaching a woman whose car had broken down and pretending to repair her vehicle. He had attacked her, but the woman had fought him off and taken Chidgey's registration number, from which he was traced by police. In his defence, he said that before the attack he had been watching porn films at an adult cinema and had become sexually aroused. He pleaded guilty and was sentenced to four years in prison. He had escaped the immediate attention of police investigating Heather's murder because he was not on the sex offenders' register, the attempted rape having taken place too long ago to place him on that list.

Ten years earlier, in 1973, Chidgey had married and he and his wife, Linda, had three children – two daughters and a son. In 1999 Chidgey left his wife for another woman in Birmingham, but returned home by the end of the year. He had various jobs, mainly as a driver for various firms, and over the years he would often disappear from his family home, sometimes for days at a time.

The final twist, however, was the manner in which

Chidgey came to be unmasked as the killer. The key figure in the breakthrough was his 18-year-old daughter Lindsey. In the aftermath of the crime she had told colleagues at Partners stationery store in Tamworth that her father had a previous conviction for attempted rape and had been missing from home at the time of the murder.

Just 48 hours after Heather's body was discovered, Detective Sergeant John Bloor had received a telephone call in the murder incident room. It was from Cindy Stanley, area manager for Partners, who related details of that conversation. Mr Bloor immediately went to the shop and spoke to Lindsey. That night he went to the family home and during a heart-to-heart with the girl, her mother and her brother Martin, a strange story began to unfold.

Although Chidgey had been married to Linda for 27 years he regularly went walkabout when he became stressed and often he would not turn up for 24 hours. Within hours of Heather's body being discovered on the Saturday morning, he had turned up, soaking wet and exhausted, and gone to bed. The next day, he had left after a row with his former wife but telephoned twice, begging to be allowed home.

His ex-wife, Linda, told the police that she had been 'very worried' Chidgey was the killer. She had confronted him and had not been satisfied by his denial. The family then told the police of Chidgey's record of sex offences, including the attempted rape in Birmingham 17 years before.

By a stroke of good fortune Mr Bloor was still in the house when Chidgey rang home again and the detective told him that, although he was not a suspect, it would be helpful to eliminate him from the investigation. Chidgey turned up as arranged at Tamworth police station and, crucially, agreed to give the DNA sample that was to prove to be his downfall. Once the samples were examined by the Forensic Science Service in Birmingham, it was found they matched the sample found on Heather's breasts and there was enough evidence to charge him.

The jury also heard that Chidgey had made a host of obscene calls to women from his mobile telephone on the days before and after the murder. Heather's mother said later: 'If he had got harsher sentences for his previous convictions, maybe Heather would still be here today.'

Sentencing the killer to life imprisonment, Mr Justice Poole told him: 'Michael Chidgey, yours was the ruthless murder of an innocent girl aged 17 entirely for your own gratification. You have taken a young life full of promise. You have inflicted an untold pain on her family and friends. You showed no pity and no remorse.'

After the case, Detective Superintendent Hall said: 'Heather's only contribution to her fate was to be a pretty young girl in a public park on a summer's evening.' He said Chidgey did not know Heather in any way and she had not been raped. But he said damage to her underwear was consistent with its forced removal and there was evidence of a sexual motive to the crime. 'Chidgey did wear women's clothing and he had an abnormal interest in women's clothes. It was not something he discussed with anyone.'

Mr Hall also said Chidgey should never be freed and paid tribute to Heather's family. 'She had her life cruelly snuffed out. It's just pure evil. I can't see a time this side of senility or infirmity when it will be safe to release Michael Chidgey.'

Just over a year after Heather was murdered, the team responsible for tracking the killer down were presented with awards by Staffordshire's Chief Constable, John Gifford. They were the Tamworth-based Sergeant Ian Coxhead, DC Dave Morris, PC Emma Dams, scientific support officer Peter Jobling, DS Peter Hall, DI Graham Ingley, DS Peter Wyatt, DC Michael Parker, DC Adrian Pustowka, PC Stafford Brooks, Margaret Kirk and doctors Jonathan Whitaker and Jane Wassell.

But the final word should be left to Heather's family, who, on the anniversary of her death, encapsulated the loss of any parents and siblings for a loved one: 'Twelve months ago you left this life and our hearts were truly broken. We think about you every minute of every hour of every day. You were so beautiful and full of life, it's so hard to believe you are gone. Life is just not the same without you.'

18

CAUGHT...
33 YEARS ON

A brief story in *The Times* newspaper in December 1991 about a 'long-forgotten' murder could hardly be described as the most sensational stories of that year, or even that day. The story, by the newspaper's science editor, recalled a murder more than two decades earlier that had horrified the nation. All murders are ghastly, but the taking of a child's life by an unknown man simply seeking some form of sexual pleasure is a crime that most people cannot even comprehend.

The paper's matter-of-fact report read: 'Surrey Police are to use a new genetic technique to try to solve a murder mystery that has been on the files for 23 years. In April 1968, Roy Tutill, a schoolboy aged 14, was picked up by a car when hitchhiking home from Kingston Grammar School. Three days later his body was found in a beech plantation beside a private road on the late Lord Beaverbrook's Cherkley Court estate at Mickleham, Surrey. He had been sexually assaulted and strangled.'

But now *The Times* added: 'All Roy's clothing has been stored for the past 23 years, and has now been sent to the Home Office forensic science laboratory at Aldermaston, where scientists will use a technique called Polymerase Chain Reaction (PCR) to multiply minute traces of body fluids in order to create sufficient DNA to produce a genetic fingerprint which could be matched against the suspect. The technique is highly sensitive, and has been used to identify DNA from prehistoric fragments of leaf, and from archaeological samples. The risk is that it is so sensitive that it can multiply contamination even a trace of sweat put on to the sample accidentally during handling. Scientists are confident, however, that it will produce a genetic fingerprint able to identify Roy's killer.'

The breakthrough did not come, however, as the technique did not give the required result, but semen stains on the youngster's clothes were extracted and kept in a freezer. Five years later SGMplus (Second Generation Profiling Plus) – which can expand tiny DNA samples for a better analysis – was used and a good DNA profile was at last obtained and loaded onto the National DNA Database. But although police now had the murderer's DNA profile, they had no match for their sample. Roy's killer was still free to walk the streets – assuming he was still alive.

Fast-forward to autumn 1999, when a father of three who had been drinking in a Birmingham pub was routinely stopped by police while driving off to his home in genteel

Solihull area to the south of the city. The man, farm worker Brian Field, appeared before Birmingham magistrates in October that year, and was convicted of drink-driving, driving without a licence, insurance or MOT and fined £150. Crucially, a buccal swab – from the cheek – had been taken from Field and it was that sample that was eventually to be analysed in the hunt for Roy's killer.

Not long afterwards, in early 2001, a team of veteran detectives were recalled from retirement to try again to solve the baffling 1968 murder. They included Paddy Doyle, former head of CID in Dorking, who had headed the original investigation and now flew in from Ireland, where he had retired 25 years earlier. The crime had attracted nationwide headlines and more than 10,000 people had been interviewed and 2,000 written statements taken.

Now Detective Superintendent Dave Cook, head of Surrey CID, was determined to catch the killer and an incident room was opened at Staines police station. Mr Cook said: 'This murder has caused a tremendous amount of emotion. It was a very high-profile case that has never been solved. Roy Tutill's blazer and the books he was carrying have been carefully kept and it brings tears to the eyes just to look at them and think what that poor young boy went through.

'We have reopened the case because methods of investigation have moved on and we are hopeful that looking at it again will reveal something that was missed at the time. The knowledge of the officers who worked on the original inquiry could be invaluable that is why I have invited them all back to help. I have written to more than 60 of them I am expecting at least 25. We have figured that some lines of inquiry may benefit from re-examination. We will be taking the old investigation to bits then building it up again to see what happened then and how our new methods of investigation can come up with a different result.

'The former officers are very keen to be involved, particularly Detective Inspector Doyle who made it his life's work to catch the killers of Roy Tutill. It was a great regret to him that he retired without them being brought to justice and it remains the county's only unsolved child murder. Some of Roy Tutill's family are still alive and we owe it to them and to the people of Surrey to get a result.'

Factors such as the use of language in the witness statements and the roads in the area had changed in 33 years, he said. 'I can't go back to 1968 so I'm trying to bring a part of it forward to 2001.'

Roy had last been seen alive on Tuesday, 23 April 1968 as he attempted to hitch a lift home from Kingston Grammar School. Dressed in his smart red-and-grey striped blazer, he caught a 65 bus to the White Hart pub in Hook. Scholarship-winning Roy – 'Tutts' to his pals – was trying to save money for a new bicycle and a train set by hitching the rest of the way back to Brockham, near Dorking, where he lived with his parents, elder brother Colin and sister Margaret. He was then spotted walking to Leatherhead Road, and seen by a bus driver trying to get a lift. A woman later revealed she had stopped the boy to scold him for hitching.

His body was found, fully clothed, in a copse at Givons

Grove, Leatherhead, near the driveway to Lord Beaverbook's estate. His blazer had been thrown over his heavily bruised body, and his leather satchel containing a raincoat and his homework was by his side. The pathologist who examined the body concluded that the boy had been strangled with a ligature. He had probably been murdered at another location and driven to the isolated spot and dumped.

Among the earlier theories was that Roy had been murdered by a paedophile ring. Two years after the investigation began, police revealed a piece of cotton had been found across his face, suggesting he had been wrapped in a curtain and kept in a car boot for some days.

Rewind now to 1936, when Brian Field was born in Bourne, Lincolnshire – only to be abandoned by his prostitute mother a day later. In due course he was adopted and grew up in a house with 12 foster boys. His new father, social worker Paul Field, would be honoured by the Queen for his work with children and even appeared with his family on an early edition of *This Is Your Life*.

By 1959, Field had joined the Royal Marines, with whom he spent two years in Malta and Cyprus and it was during this period that he had his first homosexual encounter. After leaving the services he settled in Thames Ditton, Surrey, and worked for the Milk Marketing Board as an engineer. He married twice and fathered three children. His first wife, Celia, died in a road crash in 1966 and his second, Mary, would divorce him after his pursuit of sex with boys came to the attention of police.

The year after Roy's murder Field was convicted of

attempted gross indecency, and was fined £20 by Wrexham magistrates. Three years later, he was locked up for two years after the attempted abduction and indecent assault of a 14-year-old boy in Aberdeen and it was at this point that the detectives from Surrey went to question him about Roy's death. He denied all knowledge and the police were unable to link him to the murder.

After he had served his sentence Field continued with his warped predilection. There were convictions for indecency in Oswestry and Shrewsbury before on 4 June 1986, he was found guilty at Stafford Crown Court of two counts of kidnap that bore chilling similarities to the Tutill case. He had given a lift to two boys, aged 13 and 16, and then kept them in the car. They were threatened and forced to strip before – unlike Roy – escaping from the moving vehicle. Field was jailed for four years.

Field then moved to Solihull and worked as a gardener for cash. He never claimed benefits or paid tax throughout the nineties when he became a regular at The Old Colonial pub. Ralph Newnes, the then landlord, was to say later that Field would visit the pub two or three times a week for quizzes and to play chess with a friend. 'Brian was very popular and everyone knew him as being a nice guy. I find it very difficult to relate the man I knew with the things I now know he's done. It seems impossible. He was always ultra polite and friendly and was very knowledgeable. He used to come in every Tuesday for quiz night and people always wanted him on their team because he knew so much. Brian's well spoken, well educated and a very, very clever man.'

All those visits to the pub were made on borrowed time, though, as when the detectives from the original enquiry reopened the Tutill case, all the exhibits were resubmitted for forensic tests. The advances in DNA techniques meant the killer's unique profile – taken from the boy's body – was now available.

Forensic Science Service scientist Kamala De Soyza had spent a decade trying to unlock the DNA evidence from samples retained from the original scene. As DNA techniques were refined, she would periodically use them to test for forensic evidence from semen stains left on a pair of trousers and swabs taken from Roy's body. Once she had Field's DNA from the cheek swab De Soyza was able to show that there was a one-in-a-billion chance of it not being Field.

'We were just waiting for the new techniques to be developed,' she was to say. 'The case came to me in 1991 when we looked at some of the items already examined with a view to trying to obtain DNA. We did the tests with new techniques and it proved the results and matched it to Brian Field. One Saturday in February [2001] I was able to give the results to the investigating team to say we had a match.'

Detectives then went to see Field, who by now was sharing a house with a man who had no idea of his past. One detective said: 'He was very chatty. Then we asked him if he would mind giving some blood or hair for a DNA test. He slept on it and said the next day, "I have been telling lies. I murdered Roy Tutill." It was perhaps a cathartic moment, a time to finally unburden himself of what he had done to an innocent boy.'

It must be said that the February arrest came at least 14 months after forensic scientists had sent the DNA sample from the drink-drive case. Detective Chief Superintendent Cook was to say: 'We are not in a position to say exactly what happened. Being unable to identify what the breakdown was means it is a case of learning lessons and making sure it won't happen again. We made inquiries to the Forensic Science Service and they stated that they had sent the match in 1999, but in Surrey we can find no notice of that. I am concerned about it but we are not in a position to identify where the breakdown in communication lay.'

Mr Cook went on to say he had no evidence to suggest Field had committed any crimes while free and the important fact was that he had been convicted.

That conviction came at the Old Bailey in November 2001 when Field, now 65, pleaded guilty to the murder of poor 'Tutts'. It emerged that the boy had thumbed a ride at a roundabout in Chessington at about 4pm – in a Mini driven by Field. The farm worker, whose wife had just given birth to their son, had only just restarted work and had been drinking heavily that day. He pulled into a lay-by and forced Roy to take off his clothes and perform a sex act. He set off again, only to stop in another lay-by and it was there that he strangled him with a rope. 'He just sort of convulsed a bit, sort of gasping for air and I just carried on and suddenly he went lifeless,' he was to say years later.

The murderer then put the boy's lifeless body into the boot and drove home. Three days later, as a nationwide search for the boy was underway, he dumped the body in a country lane, where it was soon found. Field lived just ten miles away from the Tutills' home.

After the killer had been sentenced to life imprisonment, Mr Cook said: 'It gives me a great sense of relief to know that Brian Field has been brought to justice. He is an extremely dangerous man. The investigation into his activities will go on to determine the full extent of his criminal past.'

That meant investigating, among others, the disappearances of David Spencer, 13, and Patrick Warren, 11, who were last seen in Chelmsley Wood, near Field's home, on Boxing Day 1996. Police also looked again at the death of 15-year-old Mark Billington found hanged from a tree seven miles from his home in the south of Birmingham, again near to where Field was living at the time.

Another man in court to see Field sentenced was Detective Superintendent Paddy Doyle, the officer originally in charge of the case and by now 85. When he had retired, his last act had been to see Roy's parents and apologise for not catching the boy's killer. As Field was led to the cells, he said he was sorry the parents 'were not here to see this day. They were devastated by his death. What can you say about parents whose child has been murdered?'

The 33 years between committing the crime and conviction was a legal record and sadly in that time Roy's parents, Hilary and Dennis, had died. His brother and sister had both emigrated. Roy's aunt, Monique Guerin, said: 'Everybody went into their own personal grief and communication between the family was lost. Christmases and so on were never the same again.'

Colin Tutill, who had passed near the spot Roy vanished from on the day he was abducted, admitted to still feeling guilt that he somehow he wasn't able to protect his brother that day. 'I don't know how it affected Dad because he kept expressions inside. At the time of Roy's death Mother was very weepy. For the rest of her life, there was a photo of Roy beside her bed. It was like a shrine. The first year or so I wanted revenge. But things evolve and that emotion is not there anymore. I always imagined if it had not been solved in the early stages, it was not going to be solved. But I'm grateful to the police for never giving up.'

19

MASSACRE AT
THE FARM

Genetic fingerprinting traps the guilty – but DNA evidence can also free the innocent.

The ground-breaking case of double-murderer Colin Pitchfork in the 1980s was the first proof of this principle. Pitchfork's arrest and conviction for slaying two 15-year-old girls only came about because DNA examination by Professor Alec Jeffreys and his team proved that a young man who had 'confessed' to one of the murders couldn't have done it. He walked free from court and the hunt was on again for the real killer, ending when police tracked Pitchfork down.

So it was that mass killer Jeremy Bamber decided that DNA could help clear him of the crime he had always denied committing. It was a desperate roll of the dice for Bamber in his quest to be free, but one that was ultimately to fail and yet again brand him a murderer.

Bamber's hopes of walking free rested on the blood-stained silencer for the rifle used in one of the most infamous slayings in British criminal history. It was in the small hours of the morning of 7 August 1985 that Bamber called police to tell them 'My father's just phoned me. He said "Please come over. Your sister has gone crazy and has got a gun"'. It was the start of the saga of the farmhouse massacre, headline-hitting in its day and still a cause of controversy almost a quarter of a century later.

Nevill Bamber, a magistrate and former fighter pilot who had become a farmer, and his wife June had moved into White House Farm in the village of Tolleshunt D'Arcy in Essex soon after their marriage in the late 1940s. They could not have children and so they adopted a son and a daughter through the Church of England Children's Society. The boy and girl, Jeremy and Sheila, were unrelated to each other. The Bambers had the pair privately educated while they could enjoy the pleasures of a middle-class upbringing in the Home Counties: Jeremy eventually started working for his father's farm while Sheila went to secretarial college before becoming a model in London, where her doe-eyed looks earned her the nickname 'Bambi'.

She married potter Colin Caffell in 1977 and two years later their twin sons, Nicholas and Daniel, were born. But the couple divorced in 1982, by which time Sheila's mental health was causing concern. A year after the divorce she was diagnosed as a paranoid schizophrenic after being admitted to a psychiatric hospital. In the meantime Jeremy, who lived in the nearby village of Goldhanger, had started dating local girl Julie Mugford.

Sheila was re-admitted to hospital five months before the farmhouse bloodbath, although she was released after a few weeks. Her sons, by now six years old, lived with their father most of the time, but on Sunday 4 August he drove them over to the farm so they could spend a few days there.

Two days later Nevill and June were said to have suggested to Sheila, who was also at the farm, that the boys should be placed in foster homes. The farm secretary telephoned the Bambers that evening and she thought she had interrupted an argument as he was 'very short' with her. It was later on that evening that Bamber said he received his father's telephone call. It would now be easy to trace and check what calls were made on landline telephones and how long they lasted, but back in the mid-1980s it was not possible.

After telephoning the police, Bamber called Julie Mugford and then headed for the farm, arriving just after the police.

They were staking the building out and no-one was allowed to go in. The tactical firearms unit arrived at 5am and two and a half hours later they stormed into the house through the back door. The scene inside the building was like a Hollywood 'gore-fest' film. Lying dead were five people: Nevill, June, Shelia, and her boys, Nicholas and Daniel.

A total of 25 shots had been fired from a .22 Anschutz semi-automatic rifle, many at close range. Nearly 40 police officers, including tactical firearms men and scenes of crime experts, attempted to sort out the carnage at the farm as Detective Chief Inspector Tom 'Taff' Jones arrived from the Chelmsford division of Essex police. Within a short time, the normally dedicated officer – who was initially in charge of the case – left the scene to play in a police charity golf match. Mr Jones, who died the next Summer when he fell from a ladder at his home, had been assured that they were dealing with a clear case of four murders and suicide by the killer, Sheila 'Bambi' Caffell. It was a scenario he always insisted was the most probable, even when Bamber became the prime suspect.

Police were initially certain that Sheila had gone berserk with her father's rifle before turning the weapon upon herself. Within days all five victims had been buried or cremated after an officer reported police findings to Dr Geoffrey Tompkins, the deputy Essex coroner, and asked for the release of the bodies.

There were a series of blunders, omissions and ineptitude which would not be repeated today.

Handsome Bamber, aged 25 at the time, convinced police of his sister's guilt. His motive, it was later to emerge, was that this meant he could inherit his parents' £436,000 fortune, worth millions in today's terms, plus 300 acres of farmland.

Indeed, at his subsequent trial, but in the absence of the jury, the judge, Mr Justice Drake said: 'The perfunctory examination carried out by the police is only explicable because they thought there was nothing left to solve'. Indeed the Home Secretary of the day, Douglas Hurd, was later to announce a tightening of procedures in murder cases in the light of the Essex blunders and Robert Bunyard, the Chief Constable of Essex, ordered an internal inquiry into the handling of the case.

Officers also admitted their approach was coloured by the

view, formed within a short time of arriving at the scene, that there was nothing to do but 'mop up,' although after Bamber's subsequent arrest, police had maintained that they had continued to keep an open mind from the earliest days. It was not until more than a month had passed after the death spree did they carry out intensive house to house inquiries among the 846 villagers of Tolleshunt D'Arcy.

Among the catalogue of police blunders later highlighted were the following: They glossed over the fact that Sheila had apparently and unusually shot herself twice – once through the neck severing the jugular and once through the chin and brain; officers initially failed to find missed a gun silencer internally stained to a depth of two inches with blood; police handled and moved the gun with bare hands instead of wearing gloves to preserve fingerprints, and a hair stuck to the silencer was lost when they sent it for examination.

There were more contradictions to the initial belief that 'Bambi' was the killer.

The obvious question that was not asked was how a 5ft 7in former model could have bludgeoned her 6ft 4in father with the rifle butt, which broke under the impact of inflicting severe face and head wounds, yet somehow remain unmarked from the struggle.

Police also failed to question how with poor hand-eye co-ordination and no known experience with guns she could have fired 25 shots into the bodies of her family with unerring accuracy, and how she could have reloaded the rifle twice without damaging her immaculately manicured nails on the tough springs of the magazine or dirtying her hands with oil and discharge residue. She also had clean feet after supposedly going on a bloody rampage through the house, and this was not queried at the time.

On the day of the murders, police got Bamber's permission to remove blood-stained carpets and bedding, which they then burnt. There were other errors, including not asking Bamber for blood samples or samples from his clothes until a month after the shootings.

Staggeringly, one of the biggest blunders was that it needed the family, cousins Ann Eaton and David Boutflour, to find the vital silencer in a gun cupboard in the house, three days after the murder. It had what looked like a dried flake of blood on it. They took it to a relative's home for safekeeping and even then it took the police a further three days to collect it. It was that silencer and the forensic details and DNA traces attached to it that was to play a significant part in Bamber's vain bid to be freed some two decades later.

In the month that followed the massacre, Bamber's behaviour was strange, to say the least. He spent lavishly, went to Amsterdam and even tried to sell soft-porn pictures of Sheila from her modelling days round Fleet Street for £100,000.

More than a month later the silencer was examined again. This time a scientist found a speck of blood of the same type as Sheila's and concluded that she must have been shot while the silencer was fitted to the rifle. The question of who returned the silencer back to the cupboard was then posed, and this also meant that it would not have been possible for Sheila to have killed herself because the gun with the added silencer would have been too long for her to hold. Detective Chief Inspector Jones – he of the golf tournament – was then removed from the case.

As if these findings were not dramatic enough, there was another twist in the story.

In early September, Julie Mugford found out that Jeremy Bamber had asked out another girl for a date. She threw an ornamental box at him then slapped him. He then ended the relationship.

Four days later she went to police and said Bamber had shown no remorse over the murders and had spent freely; he seemed to be enjoying himself. Even more crucially, she said he'd talked to her before the killings about wanting to get rid of his family and speculated about committing the perfect murder. On the night of the massacre, she said, Bamber rang to say: 'It's tonight or never' adding that he'd hired a hit-man for £2,000.

When Bamber eventually appeared at Chelmsford Crown Court charged with the murders, Julie Mugord's sensational evidence was a massive part of the prosecution case. She described how Bamber came up with several ideas for killing his parents and inheriting their estate. She said that by October 1984 Bamber was saying that he wanted to get rid of his parents. 'He just said he wanted to live his own life and he wished they were all dead' she said.

Although Miss Mugford initially dismissed the conversations as idle chat, his remarks became more specific and by December Bamber allegedly had devised various methods of killing his parents. One was to slip tranquillizers into their drinks and then later to return to the farm by foot or bicycle to burn the house down, leaving the police to believe that his father had fallen asleep and dropped a cigarette, or that a log had fallen from the fire.

Miss Mugford said: 'I said they were pretty vile and foul things to say and I would rather he didn't say things like that to me. They were horrible. I also stated it was ridiculous to try to burn down the house because it would not set on fire very easily.'

Later, according to her evidence, Bamber said that if he were to kill his parents it would be by shooting, and it was at this stage that Mr Bamber first realized he could use his stepsister Sheila as a scapegoat in the plot to kill his parents. Miss Mugford said: 'Jeremy said Sheila would be a good scapegoat because she had been admitted to a mental hospital. Due to her mental illness she wasn't in control of her senses'. She also said that Bamber had told her that he had seen a copy of his parents' will and assumed that the estate would pass to him and Sheila.

Before carrying out the killings he captured farmyard rats and killed them with his hands to test his will, she added.

On the night before the murders, she said, Bamber telephoned her. 'He said that he had been thinking about the crime and it was going to be tonight or never. I replied "don't be so stupid," and disregarded what he said, but he told me I would be hearing from him later.'

At 3am she was woken by a telephone call from him in which he said 'everything going well, something is wrong at the farm. I have not had any sleep all night. Bye honey. I love you lots.'

Explaining why she didn't tell police what she knew immediately, she said: 'Initially I did not want to believe what I thought. I was scared to believe it. Jeremy said if anything happened to him it would also happen to me. He said that I could be implicated in the crime because I knew all about it.'

Miss Mugford said she came to regard Mr Bamber as the devil incarnate but she did not want to believe what her subconscious was telling her about the truth of the murders. 'The police had told me it was an open and shut case of murder and suicide by Sheila. If the police were convinced I asked myself why anyone should believe me? I didn't know what to do. I was scared, just scared. I was scared of what Jeremy would do to me. I was scared that people would think I was mad. I couldn't handle it any more. I was increasingly upset.'

Bamber had a different story to tell. He said in court that Sheila was a paranoid schizophrenic who wanted to go to Heaven and take people with her. She had contemplated suicide several times as well as being physically violent to the twins. 'She wanted to be with God. She wanted to go to Heaven. She wanted to take people with her and she wanted to save the world.'

He said there was no animosity between him and his sister but he found it difficult to cope with her bizarre behaviour in which she said she was alternatively Joan of Arc, God and the Virgin Mary, and that she wanted to lead the campaign for nuclear disarmament. He added: 'I had been told by the police about the allegations Julie was making against me and I believed she was doing that out of spite because of splitting up.'

There was also reference to the rifle silencer – the subject of the Forensic Science Service probe two decades later – which prosecutor Anthony Aldridge QC said was 'giveaway, damning evidence' that Sheila could not have killed herself.

Mr Aldridge also said the 'only obvious explanation' of how blood matching her group got there was from a shot fired with the end of the silencer against her flesh, because of the lack of blood on the outside of it. He said: 'Sheila can't have taken off the silencer because she would have been dead after the second shot. It's far more likely that someone had shot everyone with the silencer off, then when he tried to fake the suicide by placing the rifle on the body, realized she could not have shot herself. So, he removes it because there is only a small amount of blood on the outside – the size of a pinhead. He wouldn't have appreciated the giveaway, damning piece of evidence inside.'

Bamber was found guilty of the murders by a 10-2 majority verdict. Sentencing him to five life sentences, Mr Justice Drake, said, 'Your conduct in planning and carrying out the killing of five members of your family was evil almost beyond belief. It shows that you, young man though you are, have a warped, callous and evil mind concealed beneath an outwardly presentable and civilized manner'.

The judge said that the killing of any one member of his family would have been a terrible crime, especially the murder in cold blood of the twins, Nicholas and Daniel, as they slept. He added: 'I believe you did so partly out of greed because, although you were well-off for your age, you were impatient for more money and possessions. But I believe you also killed out of an arrogance in your character which made you resent any form of parental restriction or criticism of your behaviour. I believe that you wanted at once to be the master of your own life as well as to enjoy the inheritance which would have come to you in any event in the fullness of time. In imposing on you five life sentences which are fixed by law for murder I have to consider when I think it will be likely for it to be safe for you to be released from prison into the community. I find it difficult to foresee whether it will ever be safe to release into the community someone who can plan and kill five members of their family and shoot two little boys asleep in their beds.'

The money Bamber hoped to inherit did not go to him (under law he was not allowed to benefit financially from his crime) and soon he began a long fight to clear his name. There were reviews into the police handling of the case and appeals by Bamber in 1987 and 2002 which were both unsuccessful. Bamber, 41 at the time of the second appeal, sought to cast doubt on scientific evidence and made allegations of deceit against the police. He also claimed evidence that would have helped his case was deliberately withheld. The case was referred to the Court of Appeal by the Criminal Cases Review Commission, which investigates possible miscarriages of justice.

By then, as much scientific testing as possible had been carried out. The appeal court judges determined that June Bamber's DNA – but not necessarily Sheila's – was in the silencer. They added, however, that they believed there had been significant contamination of the samples and the results were meaningless. Looking at the case as a whole, they concluded in December 2002 that 'the deeper we have delved into the available evidence, the more likely it has seemed to us that the jury were right.' Bamber had hoped the new DNA testing would prove the samples were not from Sheila but his parents. If that was the case and Sheila's blood was not present, that could mean the silencer was put away after she'd used it and that she had then shot herself. The judges' ruling rebutted this view.

Bamber's defenders had always felt the parents were shot in their bedroom. June managed to cross the room before collapsing, while Nevill struggled downstairs to telephone Jeremy. Then he fought with the attacker who beat him with a rifle butt before shooting him. Sheila could have shot herself twice with the first throat wound coming from a distance of three inches. It might not have killed her instantly, but the second, fired with the barrel pressed to the skin, would have. Also, would Jeremy Bamber really have made up a weird story of a late night phone call and a sister running amok? Why not just stay in bed all night and awake to discover the horror?

They also maintained Bamber was convicted not on substantial scientific evidence but largely on his behaviour after the killings and, of course, Miss Mugford's evidence.

They also criticised the police procedure and behaviour of the time.

Five years later, in 2007, his legal team claimed he had 'conclusively' passed a lie detector test proving his innocence. Lawyer Mr. Giovanni di Stefano said Bamber was asked a series of questions, including whether he carried out the killings and the results confirmed that Bamber was 'telling the truth' and called for him to be released.

He said: 'He has conclusively passed the lie detector test. I will now be asking the Secretary of State to refer the case to the Parole Board with a view to them releasing him'. He added that he would also be making a further application to the Criminal Cases Review Commission for an appeal in the case.

Bamber's protestations of innocence over the years have unmoved many who were close to him and the slain family. Colin Caffell had a new wife and new family and was working as a sculptor. His view was: 'In his case, life must mean life. My concern is that there might be a change in the law that does allow Bamber to appeal – or worse, allow him to be released. The judge said he is one of those few convicted killers who should never be let out.'

Cousin David Boutflour also had strong views: 'Jeremy was terribly distraught through the (funeral) service and could barely walk behind the coffins. But when we were 100 yards down the road, out of sight of the cameras and other people, Jeremy looked back at us and gave the biggest grin. It was chilling. Peter, my brother-in-law, turned to me and said: "He did it, didn't he?"'

'Jeremy is clever at publicity and letting people know he's still around. The fact is the man is guilty as hell. One of the appeal judges said that the more evidence he read the more convinced he was of Jeremy's guilt. What more does he want? How many more bloody nails does he want to put in their coffins? I really wish Jeremy wasn't a murderer and liar, that he wasn't the one who killed five members of my family. But he did it and he deserves to rot in jail for it. The Criminal Cases Review Commission really need to stop being persuaded by publicity seekers. If Jeremy came out of prison, we're pretty sure he would come after us.'

And what of the 'star' witness at Bamber's trial, Julie Mugford? She married and raised a family in Canada and, as one of Bamber's appeals was being heard, remarked: 'While I fully accept that new forensic techniques could throw new light on the case I still believe he is guilty. He has a right to appeal, that is the law. It is just very hard for me to accept. I thought this was long in the past. The last few weeks have been a nightmare. As far as I am concerned nothing has changed – I sincerely believe he is guilty. Do I stand by my original story? Yes, absolutely.'

EPILOGUE

As soon as it was announced in the 1980s that thousands of men were to be 'blooded' and their DNA analysed in the hunt for the killer of Lynda Mann and Dawn Ashworth the debate began. It is one that continues to this day; how to balance the need to catch the criminals who lurk in every civilisation with that of the freedom of an individual to be protected from a Big Brother world in which the State knows all about every individual within it.

In the case of the two murdered 15 year olds, virtually everyone approached was prepared to give a sample – apart, of course, from Colin Pitchfork, the man who killed them. The capture and conviction of Pitchfork was a piece of historic work that British police themselves later rated second only to the capture of wife-murderer Dr Crippen, through the advent of wireless, in their catalogue of crime detection in the 20th century. Not only that, but the DNA results enabled the young man initially thought to be the killer to be freed. Proof, surely, of the benefits that genetic fingerprinting can bring – a guilty man convicted, an innocent man walks free. So, what's the problem?

It is simply that a nagging doubt persists. Even Sir Alec Jeffreys, the man who more than any other symbolises DNA research, was moved to comment in late 2006 in an interview with the BBC, 'the real concern I have in the UK is what I see as a sort of "mission creep". Now hundreds of thousands of entirely innocent people are populating that database, people who have come to the police's attention, for example, by being charged with a crime and subsequently released.' The samples were 'skewed socio-economically and ethnically', he said. 'In my view that is discriminatory.'

Others have an even stronger view; that somehow the State will have access to information about our backgrounds, our appearances, our propensity to suffer inherited diseases – the cure for which is one of the original reasons of research into DNA – and a host of other intimate details.

On the other hand there is a suggestion that the fairest, and most efficient, way in which this process should be administered is for everyone to have their DNA recorded. But what happens if that falls into the wrong hands; private enterprises who exploit it for gain, a Government who uses it for totalitarian purposes?

The UK Data-base is the largest in the world. It is added to at the rate of one new 'fingerprint' every 45 seconds. It is already four million-strong and counting. Suggestions to widen its scope, to make more people liable to be placed on it for the smallest 'crime' would increase its size even further. 'But surely the innocent have nothing to fear? It's only the guilty who are running scared' advocates of widening the base point out. Police and some leading legal figures praise DNA, quite rightly, as the invaluable crime-fighting aid it is. It's pointed out that many criminals, especially those who commit sexual offences, are repeat offenders so detection protects possible future victims.

Access to a larger data base would not only bring them to justice for crimes they have committed but prevent them from offending in the future. For all recorded crime, at the time of writing the detection rate is 26 per cent when there is no DNA evidence, but 40 per cent when there is a sample, according to latest Government data.

The arguments continue and will, no doubt, increase as the technology accelerates at an even more staggering speed. But perhaps the final word should be left to James Watson, the co-discoverer of the DNA double helix structure who was speaking half a century after that momentous event: 'It is not that I am insensitive to the concerns about individual privacy or to the potential for inappropriate use of genetic information, but it would make life safer,' said Nobel prize-winner Professor Watson. And he added: 'The sacrifice of this particular form of anonymity does not seem an unreasonable price to pay, provided the laws see to a strict and judicious control over access to public data. It would be harder to be a crook... If you want to make the criminal justice system more fair, what's wrong with it?'

GLOSSARY

DNA (Deoxyribo-Nucleic Acid) is the chemical found in virtually every cell in our bodies and it carries genetic information from one generation to the next, dictating physical characteristics such as hair and eye colour. This genetic information is in the form of a chemical code or language and, except for identical twins, every person's DNA is unique, inherited half from the mother and half from the father. Brothers and sisters inherit different combinations from their parents giving them differing, albeit similar, genetic 'fingerprints'. DNA can be extracted from any cells that contain a structure called the nucleus. This includes blood, semen, saliva or hair samples.

LOCI or **LOCUS** is the name given to the area or areas analysed when establishing a DNA profile.

MLP (Multi locus profiling) was the original technique devised in the UK in 1985 with a supermarket 'bar-code' appearance. It needed a comparatively large amount of biological material to produce a result and was therefore unsuitable for data-basing.

SLP (Single locus profiling) replaced MLP in 1990 locus profiling. And it was much more sensitive in building up the 'barcode' in a number of stages. Crucially it was more suitable for 'crime-stains', where the DNA is often damaged or degraded by time.

STR (Short tandem repeat) was introduced in 1994 and is the name of the type of loci used to generate a DNA profile for the National DNA Database® (NDNAD).

PCR (Polymerase chain reaction) is the biological 'photocopier' that produces millions of copies of a particular area or sequence of DNA so that there is sufficient material to analyse.

SGM (Second Generation Multiplex) is a DNA profiling system which looks at seven areas (six areas plus a sex indicator area) to give a DNA profile. The average discrimination potential for an SGM profile - the odds on it being wrong - are one in fifty million.

SGM Plus The later technique, used since 1999, for profiling DNA samples on the NDNAD. It looks at 11 areas

(10 areas plus a sex indicator area) to give a DNA profile. The average discrimination potential for an SGM Plus is one in a billion.

DNA LCN (DNA Low Copy Number) is an extension of the SGM Plus profiling technique. It is so sensitive it enables scientists to produce DNA profiles from samples containing very few cells even those too small to be visible to the naked eye.

SNPs (Single nucleotide polymorphisms) are differences in the DNA code that are found throughout the human genome including on the Y chromosome. Most occurred far back in human history so they can be used to study the major human ethnic groups.

The **FSS** (The Forensic Science Service) is a trading name of Forensic Science Service Ltd, which is a UK Government owned company. It is one of the world's leading providers of forensic science and technology services, and is the largest provider in the UK. It provides a national service for police in the UK and other agencies such as the Crown Prosecution Service, the National Crime Squad, Ministry of Defence Police, British Transport Police and HM Revenue & Customs. It also gives world-wide assistance to a number of governments and other bodies. It is, however, independent from the police service and also carries out criminal defence work.

NDNAD (The National DNA Data-base) is an intelligence data-base set up in Britain 1995. It enables buccal (mouth) scrapes, criminal justice samples, or rooted hairs, to be obtained for DNA analysis in broadly the same circumstances as fingerprints. The information derived from these can be searched against records held by or on behalf of the police. Twelve years after its inception it was widely regarded as the most comprehensive in the world and had four million profiles on it and was growing by 30,000 samples a month, with 5.2 per cent of the UK population on it, compared with, for example, America where the comparable figure was just .5 per cent. A new sample is added, on average, every 45 seconds.